Up the Rhondda!

About the book:

"John Geraint captures, with a filmmaker's eye, so many vital facets of what made the Rhondda such a cauldron of working-class culture – its sport, its religion, its music, its communal life. In so doing, he vividly brings to life the actual experience of growing up in the valley in the final days of 'King Coal'."
  – Professor Gareth Williams, historian

"In his TV programmes, his podcasts and his writing, John Geraint is a true champion of the Rhondda, its people and of all that's best in the valley's astonishing industrial and social heritage."
  **– Margaret Jervis MBE,
  Founding Ambassador, Valleys Kids**

"John's Rhondda is one of *cawl*-warm nostalgia to begin with, but as you dig deeper, like coal that turns to diamonds, these recollections sparkle with a social history of *mam fach*s, laughter and memories of the Fawr and Fach's communities that is as refreshing as a frothy coffee. This is not bad, mun, not bad at all."
  **– Siôn Tomos Owen, author, caricaturist,
  illustrator, TV & radio presenter**

"It's tempting to say that John Geraint is the rock star of Rhondda writing."
  – Nigel Buckland, lead guitarist, Peruvian Hipsters

Up the Rhondda!
A PECULIAR SORT OF *HIRAETH*

JOHN GERAINT

y Olfa

*In memoriam Margaret and David Roberts,
Mam and Dad,
who gave me the incomparable gift
of a loving Rhondda rearing.*

First impression: 2023

© Copyright John Geraint and Y Lolfa Cyf., 2023

The contents of this book are subject to copyright, and may not be reproduced by any means, mechanical or electronic, without the prior, written consent of the publishers.

The publishers wish to acknowledge
the support of the Books Council of Wales.

Cover design: Y Lolfa
Cover image: Brynhyfyd, Tylorstown
© Steve Benbow, The Photolibrary Wales / Alamy

ISBN: 978 1 80099 487 4

Published and printed in Wales
on paper from well-maintained forests by
Y Lolfa Cyf., Talybont, Ceredigion SY24 5HE
website www.ylolfa.com
e-mail ylolfa@ylolfa.com
tel 01970 832 304

Contents

	Map: Rhondda Townships	9
	Foreword (by Sophie Evans)	11
	Preface: A Peculiar Sort of *Hiraeth*	13
1	Up the Mountain A hill-walk to a magical spot that connects the Valleys to the world	16
2	Rhondda Place Names All those *llan*s, *blaen*s, *tre*s and *ynys*es explained	20
3	Ice Creams and Frothy Coffees *La dolce vita* – Rhondda-style	25
4	The Price of Coal Two stories from our house that throw light on a changing world	30
5	Will You Come to the Pictures with Me? A tale of two cinemas	35
6	Welsh A language that feels – once again – as though it belongs to us all	39
7	Cambrian The coming of spring, and a cold, cold anniversary	43
8	Rhondda Camaraderie The ties that bind us – to each other and to where we come from	47
9	Corona! Pop goes the Rhondda!	52

10	Tom Jones in Nantgwyn Street	56
	Guess what I saw on my way back to school!	
11	Porth County	59
	The agonies and ecstasies of the 'happiest days of our lives'	
12	Central Hall, Tonypandy	64
	A remarkable social gospel in times of need	
13	Phoning Home	68
	The remembrance of rings past	
14	On a Rhondda Bus	72
	And an awfully funny way to Cardiff	
15	Dai Chips: A Rhondda Time Lord	77
	History's most eccentric history teacher	
16	Treorchy's Rugby Dream	82
	An unbelievable true-life sporting vision	
17	Why It's THE Rhondda	87
	An article that's definite about the definite article	
18	Libraries Gave Us Power	91
	Rhondda's respect for literature	
19	The Promised Land	96
	A yearning for what's yet to come	
20	Gateway to the Stars	100
	The Rhondda town that's on another planet	
21	The Choir	104
	It's not always sweet harmony in the land of song	
22	Llyn Fawr	108
	A breathtaking underwater discovery	
23	Streets Ahead	112
	A walk back in time	
24	Uncle Len: The Rhondda Working Man	116
	Heroes come in all shapes and sizes	

25	Druids Close to Home The Stones at Treorchy	121
26	In the Magpie's Nest The birth of a birthplace	126
27	Railway Lines Connections I miss	131
28	Rhondda Billionaires The real wealth creators of this world	136
29	Shopping at the Kwop Personal service, public profits	141
30	Ponty The old hometown, its bridges, rocks, chains and tunes	146
31	Welsh Hills Why we ache for a level playing field	150
32	Rhondda Fach An expedition into alien territory	155
33	Treorchy: Higher and Higher A town that's always had class – and is now in a class of its own	161
34	Fair Play Inspiring a new generation of sporting talent	166
35	Black Tips and Pyramids High places, high risks	171
36	Our Field of Dreams A state-of-the-art sports stadium – and a victorious community campaign	176
37	The Record Shop An education in popular music	182
38	We Beat the All Blacks! Rhondda rugby stars who really did	187

39	Tonypandy Riots! The Cambrian Combine Dispute of 1910	193
40	Penrhys Now a hilltop estate – once a flashpoint during Henry VIII's break with Rome	205
41	The Man Who Made Tommy Farr The mentor who guided a Welsh icon to within a punch of the World Championship	210
42	Sunday School Lessons for life	215
43	Trimming the Coalface for Christmas An illuminating seasonal tale from deep underground	219
	Postscript: Legacy, Heritage and History	226
	Acknowledgements	228

Rhondda Townships

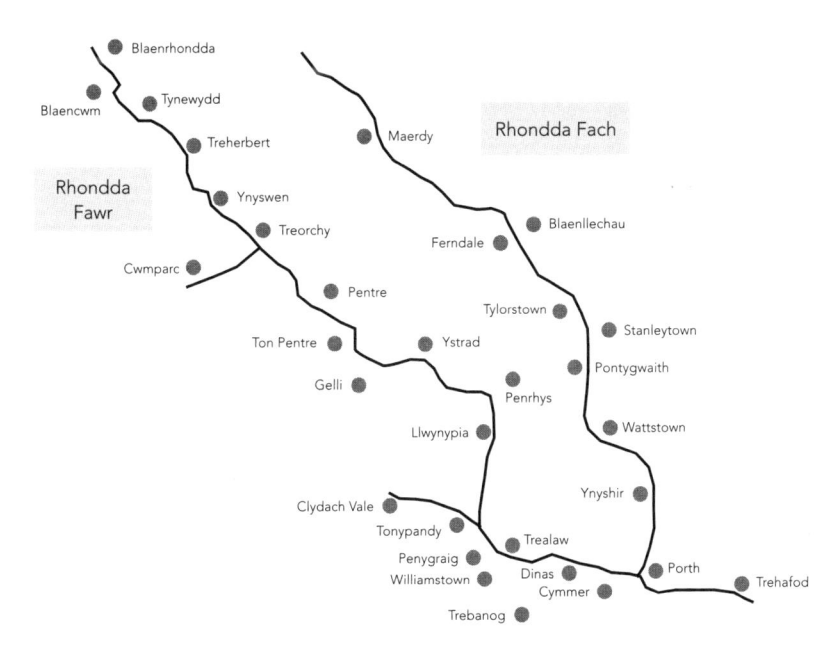

Foreword

by West End singing star Sophie Evans

GROWING UP IN Tonypandy, I always had a sense that I came from somewhere special. The shape of the valley itself, the rows of terraced houses and the hills they clung to – that was all so familiar that I took it for granted, I suppose. But the people, the sense of togetherness, of closeness that we shared, of caring for and about each other: there was no mistaking that that was something that made the Rhondda different. And when I began to find success as a singer on BBC 1's *Over The Rainbow*, I experienced the thrill of having that whole community – my community – behind me, supporting me through all the twists and turns of a big, big TV talent show.

In the same year as *Over The Rainbow*, 2010, John Geraint invited me to take part in a documentary he was directing for the BBC to mark the centenary of the Tonypandy Riots. And it was in making that programme that I began to realise much more about the history of my hometown, and why it was so special. We filmed a conversation I had with my lovely grandparents, Diane and Haydn Hill, about their memories of the heyday of 'King Coal' in the Rhondda, about the miners and their families, and the struggle for a living wage and a fairer world.

And then I got into period costume: a gorgeous purple dress, a picture hat topped by an ostrich feather, and a pair of lace-up boots – the flamboyant finery of an Edwardian Music Hall star. John had asked me to perform a cheeky song composed by the colliers of 1910, a parody of one of the big hits of the day. The miners' version was sung in the streets of Tonypandy (and in its Music Halls too, I suppose!) to celebrate and embrace the new-found notoriety that the Cambrian Combine Dispute had brought them:

> Every nice girl loves a collier in the Rhondda valley war.
> Every nice girl loves a striker 'cos you know what strikers are.
> In Tonypandy, they're very handy... with their sticks and stones and boots!
> Walking down the street with Jane, breaking every windowpane –
> That's loot! That's loot!

We had great fun filming this with a brass band at Treorchy's wonderful Park and Dare Theatre, an auditorium built with the pennies donated by Rhondda miners from each pound of their wages. The Park and Dare is the very place where my singing career began, as a small child, in *Annie*. And returning there for John's film taught me that, wherever I perform – even on the grandest West End stage – I am privileged to be part of a musical tradition, a heritage that's made the Rhondda world-famous as 'the Valley of Song'.

Music is just one aspect of our valley's rich, rich history, which John Geraint writes about in such detail and with such love in this compilation of his podcast talks. As he ranges from sport to religion, and from schooldays to shopping, the values celebrated in these chapters make me understand why I feel so proud to come from the Rhondda, and why I'm justified in feeling that pride. As the saying goes, if you don't know where you come from, how can you tell where you're going?

Wherever you're from, you won't fail to be moved, inspired, challenged and entertained by the wealth of the storytelling that follows.

PREFACE

A Peculiar Sort of *Hiraeth*

EARLY VICTORIAN TRAVELLERS to the Rhondda – which would become the most famous of all Welsh mining valleys – were overwhelmed by its sublime beauty. But beneath this scarcely populated rural paradise lay the world's finest steam coal. Within a generation of its discovery, the Rhondda had been utterly transformed. Bare moorland still enfolded it, but every inch of the valley floor was colonised by voracious, swaggering humanity. By the time of the Great War, well over 150,000 souls had poured into this cauldron, a rate of growth rivalled worldwide only by New York and Chicago.

This new 'American' Rhondda was a linear city: twelve miles long, running north to south from Blaenrhondda to Trehafod; another eight miles forking north-east from the 'gateway' of Porth up to Maerdy. A linear city in a thoroughly modern milieu: trendy shopping emporia, top-class entertainment venues, state-of-the-art sports stadia and a network of electric tramcars running the length of the twin valleys. Add to that a heady mix of progressive education, religious fervour, and articulate, radical politics. There was music in the cafés at night (as well as in the chapels) and revolution in the air.

The industrial disputes of the 1920s and the Depression of the 1930s knocked the stuffing out of all that. Joblessness visited the Rhondda. Poverty. Hunger. It became 'Heartbreak

Up the Rhondda!

Valley'. The Second World War saw a brief uptick, but by the time I was born, in 1957, only a dozen or so of the Rhondda's 79 mines were still cutting coal. So I grew up in a strange, partly ruined but once-mighty metropolis. The river still ran black through it, despite the worked-out seams of the Black Diamond. There was deprivation. Delinquency. Dereliction all over the shop. All over the shops.

And yet, and yet...

The Rhondda of my childhood still sang with a brio that was far more than plain defiance. The communal values of looking out for each other, standing by each other, standing with each other had been imprinted deep. Hard work and hard times forged our temperaments, fired our souls. Rhondda people shared a bond, a camaraderie that seemed so natural to us, but was so hard-won. In its struggles and campaigns, this valley had glimpsed a better way of organising the world, a fairer, more noble way of living, and it did more than remember it: it lived it still. It ached for fair play.

But Rhondda's egalitarianism was never content to be reduced to a flat, standardised formula for sharing out the world's miserable pittance. One of the things I've always loved about my valley is how colourful it was, how colourful it is. *How Green Was My Valley*? It was never just green. And it still is every shade of the rainbow. Full of character, full of characters. It's seen dark days and troubled times, for sure, but it's always risen above them. There's another side to the Rhondda, you see. The bizarre, the absurd, the joyful: everything that lifts life here out of the drab and the grey. The *hwyl*, the carnival of Valleys life. Brass bands and jazz bands, streaky snooker players and dead-eye darters, jokers and dreamers, painters and popstars, harpists and champion leek-growers. And my Uncle Len. The surreal black comedy of the whole shooting match. All of this, and more, is what life in the Rhondda is made of. Forget any of it, and you diminish it all.

For the last year and more, I've been ruminating on this, entertaining the people of my native valley on Rhondda Radio with a weekly talk which doubles up as a podcast – *John on the Rhondda*. I've just finished recording the hundredth edition of these popular ten-minute reflections: a 'Tonypandy Ton Up', as I dubbed the centenary episode – stealing the title of a ballad I wrote as a teenager, which I dreamt would one day be recognised as The Great Rhondda Rock Song.

Almost every week, listeners to *John on the Rhondda* ask whether my anecdotes and histories have been anthologised. In this compendium, they have their wish. Many of the chapters that follow draw on memories of those childhood and teenage years, and inevitably that involves a degree of nostalgia. But I'd like to think that this collection of *John on the Rhondda* scripts is more than a catalogue of *hiraeth*; that it coalesces as a picture of Rhondda dynamism, as a portrait of a people who have agency. It's about the values the valley has invented and imagined, the values it's lived by; and about how some of those values might help guide not just the Rhondda but perhaps the whole nation – the whole of humanity, even – towards a better future.

Whether you come from the Rhondda or elsewhere in the Valleys, or your family did, or you simply want to understand this very special community better, I hope you'll find something in what I have to say to pique your interest, and something to set you thinking about your Wales, our Wales, your world, our world. As I say in one of the pieces collected here, if there is *hiraeth* bound up in this, it's not solely that deep and characteristically Welsh longing for a past or a place that we can never enjoy again. Mine is a peculiar sort of *hiraeth*: a *hiraeth* for what might yet be.

1
Up the Mountain

WILL YOU COME for a walk with me? Come on, let's pretend that we're teenagers again, you and me. We'll head up the mountain. There's a place up there – 'Carncelyn' I call it, though 'Mynydd Penygraig' is what it says on the maps – that's got something really special about, something magical, something you'll hardly believe. I'm not sure I believe it myself.

We'll set off from my old family home on Tylacelyn Road, just below Penygraig Rugby Club. Let's go the back way: up the garden steps, out into the back lane, up the *gwli*, all along Hughes Street, to the bottom of Gilfach Road. You'll feel the steep gradient start to burn in your leg muscles now, but we can count off the side streets as we climb past them: Penmaesglas, Wyndham, Mikado, Penpisgah, Thomas Street...

Phew! Have a whiff, because there's lots more climbing to do: up that rough and twisting lane, in between the dry-stone walls – a little bit of pre-Industrial Rhondda – and out onto the bare mountain itself. This is the ridge where Carncelyn Farm once stood. A century ago, we'd have seen the boxer Tom Thomas here, training for another bout – sparring with a bull, or so they said.

When I was a boy – *which was less than a century ago!* – we'd have had to skirt round a huge a pyramid of coal waste at this point: the Black Tip. How many times did I slide down that Everest, nothing but a cardboard box for a toboggan? Beyond it was the Top Feeder, a gloopy, algae-infested colliery pond which was said to have sacks and sacks of unwanted puppies and kittens resting in its depths. It was used, all the same, by boys more daring than me as a summer swimming pool.

These days, we can just go straight up towards the summit on the old parish road. It's just a farmer's track really, but we used to call it 'the Roman Road' – as straight as any the Romans built, it is, though it must have been made a thousand years after the legions had left Wales. Local legend, fanciful but passed on with credulous delight by us nippers, claimed that an invading Roman army had marched down this very road to find the men of the valley below away hunting. The legionaries slaughtered the defenceless women and children, but then the men came home and slaughtered them. In some versions of the tale, the foreign raiders were Saxons, but the result was the same.

So now we've conquered the worst of the ascent. Let's stop to regain our breath. The whole sweep of Mid-Rhondda is laid out beneath us. Clydach Vale and Blaenclydach far left, then Glyncornel and Llwynypia, Pontrhondda and Tyntyla; lower Ystrad with Penrhys sitting above it; the long reach of Trealaw below the mountain opposite, from Ynyscynon down to Llethrddu Cemetery and onwards to Mount Pleasant in Porth; then back around through Dinas and Williamstown, Craig-yr-Eos crowning the closer slopes to the right; finally, directly below us, the massed terraces of Penygraig and Tonypandy. And – everywhere – houses: houses upon houses, hundreds of them. Thousands.

On a map, I like to think, Rhondda presents two fingers to the world. Two fingers, one slightly fatter and longer than the other. Two fingers, joined in a 'V'. Little Rhondda and Big Rhondda. Rhondda Fach and Rhondda Fawr. Dearest Rhondda and Rhondda the Great. What we're looking at is the knuckle of the fatter finger: Mid-Rhondda, the heart of the Rhondda Fawr.

17

Onwards. We're reaching the final crest now, so let's veer left, off the track, over the mossy grass. If it's not too damp, we can honour another childhood tradition of mine and throw ourselves down for a rest on the springy turf of a small hollow, the Crow's Nest. I remember flopping here the first time I ever made this climb, with a gang of older children from Hughes Street. It seemed like a great adventure – I'd only just started walking to school on my own. It was a hot day, and Mam had filled my toy plastic water-bottle with weak orange squash so that I wouldn't die of thirst. By the time I reached the Crow's Nest, the contents tasted more of plastic than of orange. Even now, I can still feel it coating my tongue.

But we're not finished yet: there's another hundred yards to go, up to the Triangulation pillar. Now you can see Evanstown and Garden Village and Gilfach Goch itself down below us. And southwards, the rich farmlands of the Vale of Glamorgan, the flats and office blocks of Cardiff, the coast at Barry, Aberthaw and Southerndown. And there's the Bristol Channel sparkling in the sunshine, Flat Holm and Steep Holm all ashimmer, the dark Somerset hills in plain sight on the far side.

And now, here's the thing – the thing that always gives me a thrill. We'll go right up to the Trig Point itself and touch the tapered concrete column. Now, stretch out both your arms, at the height of your shoulders and squarely to each side of your body, so that your open hands are lined up precisely with two cardinal points of the compass, east and west. Because this is a magical place. Not that we've climbed to any great height – just 1,300 feet above sea level, that's all – but there's an extraordinary fact I was always told about this spot.

If you go due east from here, on exactly this line of latitude, you'll pass the lower reaches of Gwent, run north of the Cotswolds into the flatlands of southeast England, cross the North Sea into the Netherlands and traverse a vast swathe of the Continent... all before you ever stand as high as this again. By then, you'd be in the Urals!

And strangely, in the same manner, heading due west at this precise latitude, there's no spot in Wales, the south of Ireland or eastern Canada that's as high as the place where we're standing right now, not until you come to the Rockies, thousands and thousands of miles away.

One day, I must check out whether this is actually true. Or maybe I won't. Maybe what's important is that I think it's true. With arms outstretched like this, you can believe it too. You can feel a kind of connection, if not to the whole wide world, then to enough of it to make it seem as if you're reaching out to embrace humanity in all its rich diversity.

And you're doing that from this one spot above the Rhondda.

2
Rhondda Place Names

WHEN YOU WERE small, did you ever write out your full, full address? You know, the complete address that located you precisely as a small child in a vast cosmos, just in case an alien spaceship was looking to deliver a parcel to you: a long list of places starting with your name and the number of your house and your street and ending something like 'Europe, The World, The Solar System, The Milky Way, The Universe'.

I remember doing that. I've a memory, too, of asking my grandfather, who lived with us and spoke some Welsh, to translate our address into English. I must have been worried that those aliens would struggle with the Welsh place names.

Apparently, our house was on Hollyhill Road, in Rocktop, near Fullingmill Meadow, up Babblingbrook Vale. Sounds awful posh, doesn't it? Like somewhere in Surrey, or the Cotswolds. The proper Rhondda version's a bit different. 'Hollyhill Road' – that's Tylacelyn. 'Rocktop' is Penygraig, of course. 'Fullingmill Meadow', believe it or not, is Tonypandy. And 'Babblingbrook Vale' – well, we'll come to that.

Rhondda place names and their meanings have always fascinated me. I was talking to someone the other day about all those ones that start with 'Tre...' – Treherbert, Treorchy, Trealaw, Trehafod, Trebanog. It led me on to thinking about why they were called what they were called, and about lots of other places in the Rhondda too.

Tre or *tref* means 'town' in Welsh. So Treherbert is 'Herbert's town'. Herbert was one of the family names of the Marquess of Bute, the lucky so-and-so who happened to lay claim to the land where they discovered the world's best steam coal in 1855. Up until then, the area was known as Cwm Saerbren. We used to call someone who was dull or lacked common sense 'a bit of a Herbert.' I'm not sure if there's any connection with the Butes. But however bright or otherwise they were, they certainly got rich from what other people dug out from underneath Treherbert.

Treorchy takes its name from the stream that flows from the mountain down into the River Rhondda there – the Gorchi or Gorchwy originally. It gave its name to the Abergorki Colliery, and so to 'Tre-orci', with the 'g' disappearing in one of those mutations that trip up so many of us as we try to learn Welsh.

Trealaw – now, that's got a nice story behind it. 'Alaw' was the bardic name of David Williams, another man who made a lot of money from coal. He bought up the land in Trealaw with the proceeds. He was a proud Welshman, very big in the Eisteddfod. There's a statue of his son, Judge Gwilym Williams, of Miskin Manor, outside the Law Courts down in Cardiff – not that I'm suggesting you've got any reason to go that way.

Trehafod takes its name from a farm. The *hafod* was the upland farm, where cattle and sheep were taken to graze in summer (*haf* in Welsh) – as opposed to the *hendre(f)*, the old ancestral winter home down in the valley. 'Hendre' crops up in local place names like Hendrecafn, Hendreforgan and Hendregwilym. Hendregwilym was translated into English as Williamstown, which caused a bit of a stir at the time. I'm not sure if the same thing happened when Glynrhedynog became Ferndale, but another Welsh coalowner, David Davis of Blaengwawr, seems to have been behind that. Tylorstown and Wattstown, on the other hand, are named after English coalowners: Alfred Tylor of Newgate in London, who bought the mineral rights to Pendyrus Farm in 1872; and Edmund

Hannay Watts of Messrs. Watts, Watts and Company. So perhaps they should have called it Wattswattstown! Stanleytown is named after a pub, the Stanley Hotel – though who the pub is named after: well, that's another matter.

As for Trebanog, *bannog* means 'high up' or 'lofty'. The Brecon Beacons, as we've been reminded recently, are properly the Bannau Brycheiniog – it's same word, *ban*: a pinnacle. High up, lofty... I bet whoever named Trebanog approached it by struggling up Cymmer Hill.

There's a whole bunch of Rhondda place names which are simple enough to understand if you know a bit of Welsh: *Pentre* – 'village'; *Dinas* – 'city' or 'hill-fort'; *Ystrad* – 'a vale', the flat floor of a valley. *Gelli* is 'a grove or copse of trees'. There were two farms near our Gelli, Gelligaled and Gellidawel: 'hard copse' and 'quiet copse', which sounds a bit like the formula for a long-running police drama series.

Tynewydd is 'new house'. Ynyshir is 'long island', like in New York – though I never heard of a cocktail called Ynyshir Iced Tea. In fact, as we're a fair step from the sea, *ynys* here (and in other Rhondda places like Ynysfeio and Ynyscynon) just means land by the river. So Ynyswen is 'white riverside'. Porth – Y Porth – is 'the gateway', which is what it is – to the Rhondda Fawr and the Rhondda Fach; and Cymmer – the Welsh word *cymer*, 'confluence' – is the spot where the two rivers meet. Maerdy is *maer-dŷ*, the mayor's house: in the Middle Ages, the 'mayor' or reeve, normally the richest farmer in the area, would oversee the landowner's estate. Penrhys means 'the head of Rhys'. Some people say it's where local bigwig Rhys ap Tewdwr was beheaded by the Normans in 1093, but I suspect that's all a bit too graphic to be true, and anyway the beheading seems to have happened in Brecon – which doesn't surprise me.

Pontygwaith means 'bridge of the work' – a small ironworks which predated the coal industry. Cwmparc is 'the valley of the park', a medieval hunting lodge. *Llwyn* means 'bush' or 'grove', so Llwyncelyn is 'holly grove'. And those of us who came into this world in Llwynypia – most Rhondda people of my generation, as I explain later – can claim we were born in the magpie's bush!

Blaen refers to the source or head of a river or stream, so Blaencwm and Blaenrhondda are the twin heads of the valley. Blaenllechau is 'the head of the Llechau brook'. Blaenclydach has always slightly puzzled me – literally, it's 'the head of the Clydach brook', but Blaenclydach is down below Clydach Vale. They always do things different up there.

So back home for me, to Penygraig – 'top of the rock' – and Tonypandy. The *Ton* bit – it crops up in Ton Pentre too – means a meadow. And the *pandy*, that's a mill – not the type used for grinding flour, but for beating wool to get rid of all the oil and dirt and to make it thicker, a process known as 'fulling'. Tonypandy's old fulling mill stood until the First World War. The hamlet near it was known historically as 'the Pandy'. The *ton* was on the other side, stretching from the old Cross Keys pub to the Clydach brook, 'the meadow near the fulling mill'.

Why does any of this matter? Well, place names tell us a little bit about the origins of where we live, about where we come from. And in my book, anyway, knowing where we've come from is a good start in trying to work out where we're going.

So, finally, what about the name 'Rhondda' itself? Proper linguists love to argue about this, but the best guess seems to be that the original name was something like Glyn Rhoddne. *Glyn* is a glen or a valley – straightforward enough. 'Rhoddne' or 'Rhoddna' – well, that's a bit more complicated and obscure, even to place-name scholars. The research and arguments about it go on, but (old romantic that I am) I'm drawn to the old explanation given by one of the pioneers in the field, Sir Ifor Williams: that the first bit, 'rhodd', may be a form of the Welsh word *adrodd*, which means to recite or to speak.

'Rhoddna' became 'Rhondda', in the kind of sound change that swaps letters around over time because... well, because it's just easier to say the word that way. So the name of our valley *may* mean 'the vale of the talkative or babbling brook'. How about that!? If it's true, it certainly fits our character: we Rhondda people are known to be fond of a good natter.

3
Ice Creams and Frothy Coffees

PARP PAH-PAH PAAAARP!... Caravaggi's! Whenever I hear it, even now, half a century later, that rhythm – long, short-short, LONG – always makes me shout "Caravaggi's!" It's a Pavlovian response. All through my childhood, it was the rhythm sounded on the horn of an ice-cream van, Nick Caravaggi's ice-cream van. The sound came from the bottom end of Hughes Street, up above our house. *Parp pah-pah PAAAARP!... Caravaggi's!*

We lived on Tylacelyn – the main road – so no ice-cream van could stop to serve cones or wafers in front of our house. But on Saturdays and summer evenings, Nick Caravaggi's regular route took him down Hughes Street. I trained myself to listen for the distant sound of the horn coming from up beyond the back lane and the council houses. *Parp pah-pah PAAAARP!...*

Those were the days before ice-cream vans had recorded jingles, before *We'll Keep a Welcome* echoed endlessly around the hillsides. Someone told me the other day that some parents tell their offspring that a jingle is the sound a van makes when it's *run out* of ice cream. How cruel can you be? Well, my mam and dad and my grandparents who lived with us knew that once I'd heard that sound – *Parp pah-pah PAAAARP!...* – I'd shout *Caravaggi's!* with such delight that they couldn't deny me sixpence for a treat.

With that shiny silver tanner in my hand, I'd rush up the garden steps, out of the back gate and pelt along the lane and up the *gwli*. Vicki Stevens, Elaine Moss and Gaynor Bowen would have got there before me, and five or six other nippers too, but the queue of expectant children was good! It made sure than Mr Caravaggi, with his Latin film star looks, was still there when I arrived – out of puff, but full of anticipation for my vanilla cornet topped with raspberry sauce.

Parp pah-pah PAAAARP!... Caravaggi's! It was a generational thing: for my children, it was Mr Creemy, not Nick Caravaggi, who served up the best ice cream in the world. I remember recording a radio feature with Mike Jenkins – Mr Creemy himself – in the late 1970s, when he'd just brought out his Christmas Pudding-flavour ice cream, which seemed insanely exotic back then. They're all grown-up now, my children, and they live away from the Rhondda, but no trip back to Penygraig is ever complete for them without a visit to Mr Creemy's or – more recently – to their new Subzero parlour in Williamstown. It's award-winning stuff, and I love the names of all those outlandish flavours – Banana-Peanut-Chocolate-Fudge, Macchiato Coffee, Amarena Cherry, Otto Biscotto... but for me there's always the ghost of Caravaggi's plain old vanilla nestling deliciously somewhere in any scoop of ice cream I taste.

Every part of the Rhondda had its own equivalent of Nick Caravaggi, selling real Italian ice cream – often licked, never beaten! Up in Ystrad it was Tich Coppolo who made a giant contribution to the happiness of local kids. Someone posted a photo of Tich on Facebook the other day, and the responses – scores of them – showed how much he and his ice-cream van were loved. "My childhood was spent looking up at him, waiting for my ice cream," said one. Someone else's typical order was "a cornet with nuts and a single off the top shelf", which I take it refers to the practice of selling cigarettes one by one. I'm not sure that happens any more, or indeed whether it did in any way declared to the authorities back then.

There are phases in growing up. The innocent wonder and sheer delight in the sight of an ice-cream cone gets replaced, sooner or later, by the need for something more sophisticated. And there's a certain awkward age – at least, there was back then – when we're too old for ice-cream vans, but still too young to go the pub. And that was when another dimension that Italians added to Rhondda life came to the fore for us: the cafés, the *Bracchis*.

A bottle of coke or a frothy coffee, a chance to sit at a corner table in a café and talk for hours with friends, with girls... That was what Rhondda café society was all about. Head and shoulders above all the other cafés for me when I was a young teenager was the Lounge Café on Tonypandy Square, known to us all as Melardi's. We'd be served by brother and sister Tereza and Tony Melardi, and Tony's new wife June.

The Melardis – Tina and Lui and Rene worked in the business too – were the children of Ernie Melardi, who'd begun to learn his trade in the café as long ago as 1920, when it was owned by one of the original pioneering Bracchi brothers, whose surname (pronounced, naturally, with a guttural Welsh 'ch') was eventually used to refer to any Italian café in the Valleys. Altogether, right across south Wales, there were said to be more than 300 Italian cafés, ice-cream parlours and fish and chip shops, almost all of them run by the families of immigrants from the northern hills of Val Ceno, around the town of Bardi.

The steam escaping from the espresso machine, the bells and buzzers of the pinball machine, the 'flipper', in the corner, the whirr of the jukebox lining up Thunderclap Newman or Bowie, T. Rex or Elton John... those were the *Sounds of the Seventies* for me. I still remember the thrill of walking into Melardi's for the first time with a couple of friends, sitting down and ordering... *a coffee!* A classic frothy coffee. That's all. It wasn't called a cappuccino back then – but, *jiw, jiw,* it felt so grown up. Bob Dylan had a song around that time, 'Tangled Up In Blue' – I'm not sure it was ever on the jukebox, but there was a line in it that went, 'there was music in the cafés at night and revolution in the air.' Well, Melardi's was our café, it played our music and our youth revolution was going to put the world to rights. We talked and talked and talked... but in the end, we satisfied ourselves with a go on the flipper.

This Penygraig kid played a mean pinball. But hard as I tried, and as much of my pocket-money as I squeezed through the silver slot for *just one more game,* I never won the weekly competition for the highest score. The grand prize of a box of chocolates put up by Tony Melardi always went to some greaser who'd mastered the art of keeping the ball in play with a series of brutal shoves to the body of the machine without ever causing a 'tilt', the penalty for which was forfeiting the whole game.

Bracchis were social centres before the term was invented: places where strangers became friends, gossip was passed on, stomachs and spirits refreshed. Regulars had a *relationship* – with other regulars, with the counter staff and with the owners. We're all social animals, and it's not just teenagers who need a warm smile, a hot meal, a steaming coffee and someone to share it with. Human contact, human connection, human kindness – that's what the Bracchis were really all about.

And there's something more. That fantastic catalogue of Rhondda Italian surnames – Melardi, Carpanini and Margaritelli, Conti and Bacchetta, Gambarini and Sterlini, Basini, Strinati, Balestrazzi: the list goes on and on like some fantastic operatic aria – there's romance in these names, yes, but they weren't simply glamorous-sounding. They were a living reminder that we were all descendants of economic migrants; that – drawn by the work and the wealth that coal generated – all of our families had arrived from elsewhere to make our Rhondda what it was, what it is. My great-grandparents might have come from Cardiganshire and North Cornelly, from Penrhyndeudraeth and Somerset and Gloucestershire, rather than Bardi. But all our families were strangers to the Rhondda once, however completely at home in the valley we felt by the time our generation was ready to taste that scrumptious ice cream for the very first time.

4
The Price of Coal

IT WAS THE minister who told the story. At Mam and Dad's Golden Wedding Anniversary, if memory serves me right. He gave a little speech at the celebration, telling everyone about the first time he'd come to the Rhondda, way back in the last century, as a prospective new pastor for Bethel Baptist chapel, Tonypandy. Dad was one of the deacons, so the nervous young candidate presented himself at our house on Tylacelyn, in the last block at the bottom of the hill, just below Penygraig Rugby Club. The would-be minister would have climbed the steep steps up from the pavement. Dad would have answered the door, saying, "Welcome, brother!" and testing him out with a firm handshake. And Mam would have *insisted* that he should have a cup of tea. But first, smiling proudly, she would have escorted him – as she did with all first-time visitors – to the front room window, so that he could admire the view. To her, it was like gazing on the Promised Land.

Our house was directly across the road from the old Naval Colliery, but that had been closed the year after I was born. The site had been cleared and partially redeveloped. In fact, one of my most vivid boyhood memories was standing in a crowd one Sunday morning outside the Rugby Club – the old Colliery Manager's house – to watch the stack, the colossal colliery chimney, being blown up and falling dramatically to earth.

So there was the young minister-to-be, looking out of our bay window at the view, Mam's view, the one she was so proud of. To the right: Graig Park, the spanking new rugby ground, laid out where the colliery spoil tip once stood. Rising behind it, Craig-yr-Eos – the Nightingale's Rock. Lovely name! Directly opposite, the imposing mass of Trealaw Mountain, covered in heather. To its left, below Penrhys, the green flanks of Tyntyla, and glinting in the last of the afternoon sun, long lines of slate roofs leading the eye northward, teasing it with a hint of the *cwm* opening up again towards Treorchy. Completing this vast panorama, the sheer slopes of Glyncornel, once bare but adorned now by the Forestry Commission's upright Scots pines (my Grampa, who'd scarcely been further than Cardiff in his long life, had always delighted in the afforestation: "*Duw*, it's just like Switzerland, mun," he'd say).

Mam *knew* that the splendour of all this would impress this pleasant young man. She waited in silence, giving him every chance to drink it all in. There was no need to gild the lily. Finally, she decided the time was right to prompt his appreciative response.

"*Beau-ti-ful* view, isn't it?" she sing-songed.

Genuinely puzzled, he replied, "It's… *a petrol station.*"

He was right, of course. Large as life, dominating the foreground, just yards away directly across the main road, was the Shell petrol station. Cars and tarmac, glass and concrete and plastic, pumps and prices and adverts and the Shell logo and all. Built on the site of the little reservoir that served as the old Naval Colliery feeder. Owned and managed by Trevor Morgan, *Mister* Morgan next door. It wasn't that Mam didn't know all of that or couldn't see it. She could; she simply screened it out in favour of the bigger picture. Perhaps it helped to have a lifelong attachment to that biblical verse, 'I will lift up mine eyes to the hills.'

The minister said later he really didn't know if she was setting some kind of test for him. His confusion opened my eyes to what I'd taken for granted. For the first time, I realised how *telling* it was: this filling station on the site of what had been a working mine, where my Grampa had been the colliery blacksmith. Where once they'd dug coal, now they pumped petrol. From this exact spot had come the black diamond that propelled warships and great ocean liners, and powered massive cargo vessels to the far ends of the earth. Now the fuel was brought here, to fill up cars for shopping trips, journeys to work, sunny-day outings to 'beauty spots': private needs, domestic, local. The world had moved on and the motive force that drove it had changed. What once upon a time the Rhondda had been – the engine-house of modernity – other places, faraway places, were now becoming: Texas, the Persian Gulf, the Oil States of the Middle East. Power had shifted.

That was what the economic crisis of my teenage years in the 1970s was all about. Oil, and the power of oil. That was why there'd been galloping inflation, why the pound had to be devalued, why Britain had to go cap in hand to the IMF, as Rhondda colliers had once had to go to the mine-owners. It was all here, right in front of me, and I'd never seen it in all the time I was growing up. King Coal was dead. Oil now ruled. *Mam fach*, there'd be an almighty struggle over it one day. The sheikhs and sultans would make sure that the wealth generated by oil stayed in their hands, stayed in their homelands (*and why not?!*). What a contrast to the fortunes that came from the coal industry, which had been sucked out of these Valleys, leaving them high and dry.

There was another story about our house which the minister didn't tell, though he'd probably heard it from Mam at some point. It happened a decade before his visit. We were getting the house *modernised*. Perhaps something similar happened to your house. The original Edwardian features, the fireplaces, covings and skirting boards were stripped out. Smart white radiators replaced the open coal fires. Artex on the ceilings. The 'back kitchen' – our cosy sitting room with its free-standing stove – was turned into a proper modern kitchenette, with made-to-measure work surfaces and built-in appliances. The lean-to bathroom, scullery and outdoor toilet were demolished: instead, a square, flat-roofed extension was purpose-built to house an up-to-the-minute bathroom suite: matching tub, sink, toilet and all. In avocado, of course. The wall between the front parlour and middle room was knocked through, with a pair of full-length sliding glass doors between the two to allow for some privacy. Whilst we were away on holiday, the builders fitted the doors with trendy tulip-patterned glass. The tulips on one door were upside down, but it was too late to do anything about that by the time we got back. Only the *cwtsh-under-the-stairs* remained as a reminder of how old-fashioned it all used to be.

One Saturday morning before all this building work had begun, Dad and I had gone up through the tiny trapdoor into the attic to measure up, so that we could fill in the form for the Loft Insulation Grant the government was offering. No-one had been up there for years, decades probably. I went first, up the homemade stepladder Grampa had put together, poking my head warily into the dark space beneath the eaves. We'd brought a torch with us. What was revealed in the beam of light was an eye-opener. Across the whole floor of the attic, from wall to wall, lying between each rafter a full six inches deep, there was already a perfectly good form of insulation. It was pitch black. It was powdery. It was coal dust.

Our house, you see, was less than 50 yards away from the upcast shaft of the Naval Colliery. The dust, expelled from the headings deep below, had been settling there every working day, ever since the house was built. Imagine putting the washing out, or trying to keep the rooms clean in an atmosphere like that. Imagine working underground.

That was the price of coal, the real price. Dust. Dust on every surface in the house. Dust on clothes, dust on skin.

Dust in the lungs of the colliers. Dust to dust they went, so many of them.

We never did get the government's insulation put up in our attic. There wasn't any point, was there? It was all thoroughly draughtproof as it stood. Sealed off by all that settled coal dust. Mind you, if our house had ever gone on fire, you'd have been able to warm your hands in Blaenrhondda.

5
Will You Come to the Pictures with Me?

Will you come to the pictures with me? To the cinema, I mean. The flicks. Oh, I know it's a bold question, but I think we know each other well enough by now. Mind you, when I was a teenager, it would take me weeks to buck up the courage to ask a girl that question: *Come to the pictures, for a date?*

Let me ask you something less awkward, then, instead – one of those security questions they ask you to prove your identity these days. *What was the first film you ever saw in the cinema?* I'll never forget mine.

We lived with my grandparents, and they disapproved of the cinema, as many older chapel people did in the Rhondda. It was the Devil's Work, like alcohol and playing cards and Sunday newspapers. So what were the chances that my first film was called *Dr Syn? Dr Syn, Alias the Scarecrow*. You see, one Saturday, my older cousins Susan and Pauline were looking after me, and they were determined to see this film that was showing in the Plaza in Tonypandy. It was a period piece, the film version of a TV series. Patrick McGoohan stars as the Scarecrow, a masked rider fighting in disguise for the poor villagers of Romney Marsh, against the king's harsh taxes and the naval press gangs. It's a Walt Disney production, so it can't have been a proper horror movie, but it scared the living daylights out of me. All those galloping horses, shot in silhouette, and guns and sharp swords, and hiding from soldiers in creepy barns. And the cinema itself was dark and creepy when the lights went down, which I wasn't expecting. I sat between Susan and Pauline, holding their hands, trying not to cry. But as soon as the film finished, they took me to Hathaway's for chips, and I felt *loads* better.

There were two cinemas in Tonypandy in those days. The Plaza, at the bottom of Dunraven Street by the traffic lights, and another one on Pandy Square called the Pictured Room. The room with pictures. Made sense. It was years before I realised that it was actually *the Picturedrome*. Like Aerodrome. Or Hippodrome, I suppose: I'd never heard of one of those, though it turns out that it was the original name of the Plaza.

The Plaza and the Picturedrome. One of them always seemed to be showing *Zulu*. All the boys went to see it dozens of times. Then we'd re-enact the battles on the tumps at end of Hughes Street, never failing to quote the famous line, "Zulus... to the south-west! Thousands of 'em!" Though it was all shot in South Africa, it's a very Welsh film – Ivor Emmanuel rallying his comrades with a rousing 'Men of Harlech'. The producer and star of it all, of course, was Ferndale's own Stanley Baker. A great actor, held in awe by his fellow professionals. When he died, far too young, his friend Richard Burton said that there was "a class of Welshman, original and unique to themselves, powerful and loud and dangerous and clever, and they are almost all South Welshmen and almost all from the Rhondda Valley" and how there weren't enough of them, so few that we couldn't afford to lose any, and how it wasn't fair that another one had been taken away. Some obituary!

Some weeks, the Plaza and the Picturedrome would *both* be showing X-rated films. Nothing terribly explicit: more violence than sex, usually. But that didn't stop us young teenagers wanting our weekly fix of movie magic. And the cinemas were reluctant to turn customers away. So we always got in, even though we were clearly underage. One of the boys – I'll call him Titch – was so small and underfed that he used to be let in for half price on a child's ticket. We'd find an empty row and settle down to the familiar pattern: the B movie first, and then the famous Pearl & Dean adverts before the main feature. I do remember newsreels, but I was too young to witness the legendary occasions when Winston Churchill's appearance in them was booed to the rafters. A war hero elsewhere in Britain, Churchill was never forgiven by Tonypandy for sending in the troops to break the miners' strike in 1910.

When I was a bit older, my schoolfriends organised an outing to see *Ben Hur* at the Picturedrome. One of them, Geoff – a bit of character – had come all the way down from the top of the valley. He couldn't restrain himself any longer than the first few scenes before announcing his presence to the whole cinema. The Roman army was marching through Nazareth. The centurion asks, "What village is this?" And Geoff pipes up, loud enough for the entire cinema to hear, "BLAENRHONDDA!" Mild amusement in half the packed house. Severe displeasure in the more mature half. But by the time it came to Crucifixion scene, a subdued Geoff was weeping openly. "I wouldn't have come," he sobbed, "if I'd known God was going to be in it."

When I got a little older still, I knew I should be asking girls that awkward question, *Will you come to the pictures with me?* I wasn't the kind of boy that girls swooned over, but at long last I surprised everyone, myself included, by getting a date with a gorgeous girl. She was everything a boy dreamed of – *she had the Best Legs in Sunday School!* – and she lived up in Ely Street. Before heading to the Picturedrome to meet her, I had a proper bath, and combed my hair 17 times. I even changed my socks. I hadn't started shaving, but all over my face, my neck, my best Ben Sherman shirt and my corduroy jacket, I splashed a whole bottle of Brut.

The film was a stinker too. *Take Me High*, starring Cliff Richard. It's been called "perhaps the most remarkable movie ever shot in Birmingham". It sure is no *Citizen Kane*. You'll get the idea if I say that Cliff's character opens a fast-food restaurant, and one of the twelve 'hit songs' he sings in the movie – all of which have sunk without trace – was called 'Brumburger'. Honest, now. And sad to say, *Take Me High* was probably the high point of my romantic adventures as a teenager. I still can't pass the end of Ely Street without a little shudder and a twinge of regret. I should have taken her to the Plaza.

So why did we all go there, to the pictures, week after week? Some magic drew us Rhondda kids back to the dark cocoon of the Plaza or the Picturedrome, the Central or the Gaiety, the Welfare, the Park and Dare or the Workmen's Hall. The 'torchie' – the usherette – would show us to our seats, and we'd sit, oblivious to our neighbours, and make our Great Escape – into glamour, into heroism, into the heat of battle or the fires of love, into the past or the future, forgetting about the here and now, the present, our present.

Millions of others, all over the world, were doing just the same. But when the credits rolled, it was only us who emerged, blinking, into the darkness of Tonypandy or Treorchy, Tylorstown or Porth, where – if only we'd had eyes to see it – there was more to fight for, more to love, more heroism and yes, more beauty, too, than Hollywood could ever have imagined.

6
Welsh

S*HWMAE*? D*ID YOU* go to the Welsh school? Did you send your children there? Are your grandchildren at Welsh school, perhaps? Someone you know goes there, I'll bet. Nowadays, so many families in the Rhondda, as in every other part of the country, have an active connection with the Welsh language. And that's great to see.

Back when I was in junior school, things were a bit different. On St David's Day, the girls would get dressed up in Welsh hats and shawls, the boys might wear a small cloth leek, we'd have a short concert and sing *'Calon Lan'*, maybe, and then we'd dash out of school for our half-day off – and that would be that, as far as Welshness was concerned, for the rest of the year.

Of course, it would have been different if I'd been at the Welsh school… 'the Welsh school' – it's an odd phrase, isn't it? I mean, all the schools in the Rhondda are Welsh. But back then there was only one junior school in the whole of the Rhondda Fawr that *taught* in Welsh – Ysgol Gymraeg Ynyswen. And when the Ynyswen children got to secondary school age, to continue their lessons in Welsh they had to be bussed out of the valley down to Rhydfelen, miles beyond Pontypridd.

It's fair to say that many Rhondda people thought Rhydfelen was posh, and a bit snobby. But then people said that too about Porth County Grammar School, where I went, so who am I to talk?

At Porth County, we were given the choice of two languages to learn: Welsh or French. French was a proper modern language, a language with a future, what with the Common Market and all of that. Steered by advice that it would be a boon to their careers, almost all of my class plumped for *le français*. But I was a contrary so-and-so. I chose *Cymraeg*. I reckoned I'd have a flying start with Welsh. After all, I'd been born in Llwynypia, been brought up in Penygraig, lived on Tylacelyn, gone to school in Hendrecafn, played in Penmaesglas, on Craig-yr-Eos and Carncelyn. String all those place names together and I'd have practically passed the O-level oral exam without trying! And the English we spoke, though we might not have realised it, was full of Welsh too.

"There's a *bwgi bo* up that *gwli*!"

"*Duw*, don't talk *twp*, *mun*, and gi's an *'ansh* of your apple."

When I got to my O-level year, the set poem for group recital in the Urdd Eisteddfod turned out to be '*Y Ffynhonnau*'. It means something like 'The Mountain Springs', I suppose. It's an epic poem all about the Rhondda, by Rhydwen Williams – a kaleidoscope of the valley's long history: coal mines and boxing booths, chip shops and sarsaparilla fountains, chapels and the Holy Well at Penrhys, all done by a chorus of voices speaking proper Rhondda Welsh, with a sprinkling of English phrases thrown in, naturally. So it was natural for us at Porth County to have a crack at it. And it's still one of my proudest achievements that we did it: we won First Prize in the Eisteddfod, beating Rhydfelen at their own language... 'Their own language' – there you go, another strange phrase. We did think of Welsh like that, but it was *our* language too.

I was lucky at Porth County: I had a succession of brilliant and committed Welsh teachers – Berian Davies and Delyth John, Olwen Peters and Eleanor Aubrey. Eventually, thanks to them, and a summer spent working on a farm in Carmarthenshire, I became fluent in Welsh – well, fluent enough to make TV programmes in the language, anyway. By then, Welsh had begun to flourish again in the valley. The Rhondda could boast of *five* Welsh-language junior schools – Llwyncelyn, Bronllwyn and Bodringallt, and Llyn y Forwyn in Ferndale, as well as Ynyswen – and a big comprehensive in Cymmer. Welsh was popular now, not posh.

So, in 2002, this crazy idea came to me – how about making a film where that favourite poem of mine, *Y Ffynhonnau*, got recited by *every* child who was at Welsh school in the whole Rhondda? There were hundreds and hundreds and hundreds of them. We could gather them all together on top of Penrhys where the poem begins and get them to recite it there. Madness! There wasn't even a toilet up there.

But the great thing about working in television is that people are willing to do the daftest things if they're going to be filmed. And once I managed to persuade the schools it was a good idea, the thing began to snowball. The Pendyrus Choir got involved. And the Cory Band. And loads of other top-class talents from the Rhondda: the actors Daniel Evans from Cwmparc and Judith Roberts from Ferndale; the wonderful folk singer from Treherbert, the late Siwsann George; the much-missed and legendary Penygraig rock guitarist, Tich Gwilym. All sorts of other performers came on board too – dancers and swimmers, Treorchy rugby icon Adrian Owen, Huw Davies (who taught me English!), Italian café owners and a man who kept champion racing pigeons. Clydach Vale's Glyn Houston – veteran star of TV and film and, by now, sadly, another talent who has left us – said that he wanted to be part of it, too, though he didn't speak much Welsh at all. But we gave him a few short lines, and he had such presence on the screen that he became a really big character: the retired miner who represents the very spirit of the Rhondda.

So there we all were, a thousand strong, one summer's morning, processing across Penrhys, behind the Maerdy

Miners' Lodge banner, and the Treorchy Comprehensive School band. Chances are, depending on your age, if you're from the Rhondda, you might have been with us, or your nieces and nephews were, or little Gareth or Siân from down the street, who are all grown up by now. After all, it was 20 years ago. *(Pleasingly, after these words were broadcast as a podcast, I heard again from the youngest cast member of them all, a Penygraig lad who had played a toddler being told a bedtime story by his 'Mam', Judith Roberts. He wanted a DVD of the production to watch his own performance again. He's now a professional rock musician.)*

The film made a bit of a splash at the time it was made. We had a grand premiere – just like Hollywood – in the splendid Park and Dare Theatre in Treorchy. The massive auditorium was packed out. And when – up on the big screen – those hundreds of children, all of them Welsh speakers, gathered on Penrhys in front of the Virgin Mary's statue, up above the Spring and the Holy Well, and they began to chant the poem's most famous line, *"Mae'r ffynhonnau'n fyw* (The mountain springs are alive)!", it really did feel like we were all part of something vital and thriving, something bubbling over with the zest and *hwyl* of youth – and that Welsh, too, was a language of the future here in the Rhondda.

7
Cambrian

'THE MERRY MONTH of May': it's that time of year when Rhondda people can look forward – to summer sun, warm days, long evenings to come. It was pleasant enough for a walk the other day, so I met up with one of my very best friends. Paula is as proud of her roots in Clydach Vale as I am of mine in Penygraig, and we met on her territory – we even called by to say hello to her mother. Paula's mam is one of the Rhondda's great characters, with a sharp tongue and a sparky eye. She must be in her late eighties now, but she's still as mischievous as a teenager. There are tales I could tell, though perhaps not here. Suffice to say, I call her 'The Queen of Park Street'. She's seen troubled times and come out – regally – the other side of them. And there's nothing wrong with her memory! She reminded me that when I was a teenager, I used to drop by at her house at all hours to see her daughter, claiming I was 'just passing the door' – as though the bottom of Park Street was the main thoroughfare up and down the Rhondda and someone walking there *could* be on their way to somewhere else.

Anyway, Paula and I had arranged to meet so we could take a walk around the Cwm Clydach Countryside Park, which sits on what was once the site of the Cambrian Colliery. 'This oasis of calm, wildlife and stunning views has been created from the blackened scar of a coal mine,' says the Council's website. It's true, but I wish they hadn't put it quite that way. The scenery is gorgeous and the ascent up the *cwm* from the

Bottom Lake to the Top Lake – 280 feet higher – makes for a lovely, if slightly challenging, hike. But the Council can't magic away our industrial past so easily.

Our walk took us up to the black pit wheel and the old coal tram that stand as a memorial to that past. Because 'the merry month of May' is also a time when we look back – to the darker, colder days we've lived through.

One of the May days that Clydach will always remember is Monday 17 May 1965. 31 miners were killed that day, underground in the Cambrian Colliery. It was a day when the Mines Rescue team from Dinas sped up Court Street, too late. A day when neighbours on Wern Street had their ears filled with the sirens of ambulances, their hearts chilled with fear. A day when women waited silently for news at the pit top. A day when hope failed for so many, and night came with no comfort.

I have a memory of that day. I've often wondered if it's a false memory, because I was just 7 years old in May 1965, and I was at least a mile, as the crow flies, away from the pit, out the back of my house on Tylacelyn Road in Penygraig. I used to go home from Hendrecafn Juniors for my dinner. My delicate stomach couldn't stand school meals. Or perhaps I was just spoiled. Kicking a ball around our tiny backyard, I heard a low boom which seemed to come from over towards the Incline or from further into Tonypandy. It didn't sound like much, but somehow, young as I was, it struck me as significant. Just then, Mam called me in to eat.

"What was that noise? Now just?" I asked.

Lightly, my mother passed it off, shepherding me inside. "Just a car backfiring, I expect."

Did she know? Had she heard it too? Did she realise...? Probably. She was a Rhondda woman, after all. By the time I came home again from Hendrecafn that afternoon, everyone knew. 31 souls gone. In that instant. As I'd been playing ball a mile away.

Could I really have heard the explosion? As a grown up, it's always seemed unlikely to me. But then, others who were also safe above ground that afternoon tell me that they too heard it. What's certain is that, days later, I stood with hundreds, thousands of others, lining Dunraven Street, as the dead miners' comrades processed behind the hearses, an endless line of black funeral suits and ties. The tramp of their feet was the only sound. Policemen saluted. Women stifled sobs. And the hearses took the men's bodies, united in death as they had been in their working lives, to rest in Llethrddu Cemetery, Trealaw.

Every Rhondda family will have some memory of 'the blackened scars of coal mines', and the toll they took on us. Paula's father had an elder brother. He was just 15 when he was killed in an accident when the spake, the underground trolley that took miners down to the coalface of the Gorki Drift, ran out of control. His body was brought home to be laid out on the kitchen table.

My Gransha, my dad's dad, had the blue scars of a faceworker, a coal-hewer. He turned up to work his shift at Lewis Merthyr in Trehafod one morning in 1956, and found himself part of a recovery party instead. From pit bottom, he helped to send back up that day no hard-won coal, but the burnt bodies of nine of his butties who died simply because they went to work that day. He was lucky, he said. But he was never quite the same again.

He'd been born in Clydach, my grandfather – 'Dai Clydach' was one of his nicknames. 'Dai Budgie' was the other, because he bred prizewinning canaries and budgerigars in a 'cot', or shed, that took up most of his front garden in Holborn Terrace, Tonypandy. My Auntie Marion, his daughter, kept several suitcases full of rosettes he'd won from the Tonyrefail and District Cage Bird Society.

"'Dai Clydach', 'Dai Budgie', aye, we remember him," said a group of his work butties to me – my father had arranged for me to go down underground at Lewis Merthyr on a Saturday morning when I was a student, just to see where my Gransha had worked years before.

"Aye, we remember him," repeated the small maintenance crew who were on shift. "Always looked so well, he did."

That got me. My memories of him were largely after his stroke, when he lost the ability to move one side of his body, when his butties had to come one weekend and take that 'cot' down and take his prize birds away, because he would never again be able to look after them. And I remember that, in the end, his death certificate didn't mention trauma or dust, so there was no compo for my grandmother. But we knew what he died of, all the same.

Aye, those mines have left their scars, and they're still there, no matter what the Council says, no matter how beautiful the Cambrian Lakes look in 'the merry month of May'. And we *should* remember them, those black scars, those blue scars, because they've made the Rhondda what it is: they've given us our strength of character, our sense of fair play, our willingness to look out for each other, to stand together, no matter how tough things get.

My thoughts have travelled a long way from the Queen of Park Street teasing me on her doorstep. She's seen a lot, come through a lot: one of the tens of thousands of Rhondda women who carry our collective memory of the way things went in this valley. Despite that burden, she was full of spring-like cheer as she waved us off… and she's right to be so positive. Summer's on the way.

But let's not pretend there hasn't been a winter. We'll enjoy the warmth of the season so much more if we acknowledge what we've lived through.

8

Rhondda Camaraderie

WE WENT OUT for lunch today, a gang of us. Friends, Rhondda friends, out for a celebratory meal. I've known them this ages – we first got together as teenagers at school, 50 years ago now. Back then, we loved each other to bits. And we still do. We've moved around since then, and some of us have married people from outside the Rhondda – as far afield as Pontyclun, mark you. But we remain the same, at heart. Rhondda written right through us, like a stick of rock. Not that I've ever seen a stick of rock from the Rhondda. Porthcawl, yes. But you know what I mean.

Schoolfriends. There's something about them, isn't there? When you've known them for so long. Oh, I'm not saying we haven't changed at all. We're older, for one thing. And more sophisticated. We called it *lunch*, not dinner. But that's because it was a *pub* lunch, and that's what they're called, isn't it? It's a *pub lunch* not a *pub dinner*. The food wasn't anything special, to be honest with you, and the pub was freezing, but the conversation – well, it was enough to warm the cockles of my heart.

I mean, what we said was nothing out of the ordinary: just us sitting around catching up with news about each other's families; poking fun at the way *some* Rhondda people decorate their houses these days; talking about exotic holidays we'd had (*in England!*); pinpointing precisely where the children's reading table was in 'Pandy Library years ago, and what we were reading when we sat there (*The Famous Five*, anyone?);

47

marvelling at how a classmate's father could walk up from the valley floor in Pontygwaith all the way to the top of Penrhys *when he was 102*; arguing about exactly where the posh bit of Clydach Vale is; telling silly jokes about prawns making magic wishes, and talking rabbits walking into bars. You've done the same sort of thing yourself, many times, I know you have. Well, maybe not the prawn and rabbit jokes. That bit *was* surreal, and for once it wasn't me playing the fool. But the ease with which we shared our stories, the delight we took in each other's company, the memories that sprang unbidden to mind just because we were together – all of this was precious. Even out for lunch, we were *at home* with each other, and that's priceless.

The thing about schoolfriends is there's *no pretending* with them. If you've put on any airs and graces in your old age, if you give out that you're something that you're not, they'll tell you straight. "Shurrup, mun," they'll say, "don't talk wet," or words to that effect. It's impossible to fake it when you've known each other as spotty teenagers, when you've caught the same school bus, when you've copied your homework from someone else's Rough Book, when you swapped your Deputy Head Boy's badge with your friend who was Deputy Head Girl just for a laugh, to see if anyone else noticed (they didn't!). These are people who know where I come from. And I don't just mean Penygraig. I'm an only child: they're the closest I've got to brothers and sisters.

Most of these friends at lunch had acted with me in school plays at Porth County, and that forges a special kind of bond, a bond you only get from working or performing together. Once you've experienced it, you know that there's nothing quite like it. You learn to rely on each other as you strive towards something that's not easy to achieve. Sports teams have it. So did everyone who worked underground, years ago – they had it big time! *Camaraderie* they called it, the miners. Standing by each other, standing up for each other, sharing a laugh, and a whiff, and a tear sometimes. These were tough, unsentimental men, engaged in back-breaking work. But, my goodness, they knew what they valued, and they valued what they knew. As I've said, my father's father – 'Dai Budgie' or 'Dai Clydach' to his friends, Gransha to me – was a faceworker at Lewis Merthyr colliery in Trehafod, the one that's now the Rhondda Heritage Park. He was always adamant that he didn't want his son going underground when *he* grew up – it was too hard, too dangerous. But all the same, Gransha said, if he could have his own time over again, he would choose exactly the same line of work – the fellow-feeling he found with his butties, his workmates down the pit, was worth all the world to him.

For me and my friends, staging Shakespeare's *Twelfth Night* at school meant experiencing, for a few weeks, a faint echo of that kind of camaraderie. It was an experience I've tried to capture in *The Great Welsh Auntie Novel*, a work of fiction loosely based on my teenage years which was published in 2022. For those weeks of intensive rehearsals and performance, we lived inside a metaphor, or rather we lived it out: a metaphor for an ideal society, where the 'from each' and the 'to cach' is in perfect balance. We learnt how to trust each other, to know instinctively when to improvise and when to stick to the text. We learnt to respect each other's talents and each other's feelings. How to support each other when things went wrong in front of a packed house, as inevitably they did. Mind you, when one of the girls had a make-up malfunction, it was as much as the rest of us could do to stop ourselves from corpsing. There it was – one of her spectacular false eyelashes, detaching itself and slipping slowly down her cheek, and her delivering one of Shakespeare's most romantic speeches with her head weirdly cocked to one side in a vain effort to prevent the false eyelash from falling off altogether. Good thing it was supposed to be a comedy!

Of course, we were young then, and we lived in each other's company, lived for each other, with a kind of intensity that it's impossible to maintain when life takes you in different directions, when you aren't working and playing together every day. One of *Twelfth Night*'s most famous lines is 'Youth's a stuff will not endure.' Well, that might be true, but our friendship *has* endured half a century, and that's all because of the bond that we forged back then.

Over lunch, we did talk a little bit about how the Rhondda has changed – "It's not the same, is it?" – but then we all agreed that it's still *different*: different to other places. Even to Pontyclun. There's a Rhondda joke I like to tell. It's one of those surreal ones, though it doesn't involve prawns or rabbits. It's about two blokes walking towards each other down a street in Treorchy. When they get to within talking distance, the first one says, "Not bad, mun." And the second one replies, "Alright, butt?" That's it. That's the joke.

Have I got to explain it? Alright then, though explaining it more or less kills the humour. Not that it was *all that* funny in the first place. The point is that these two men take it so much for granted that they'll acknowledge each other's presence, even though they don't really know each other, that it doesn't even matter if one of them speaks the answer before the question's asked... "Not bad, mun." "Alright, butt?"

Not everywhere is like that. The way in which Rhondda people greet passers-by in the street is special. Whoever walks past us, even if we don't know them, we *know* them, if you see what I'm getting at. It may not be unique to the Valleys, and it may not happen as often as it used to, but apart from small villages where everyone has a good idea who everyone else is, it's *exceptional*; and extraordinary in somewhere like the Rhondda, where tens of thousands of people live. It's another echo of the camaraderie that miners talked about, the camaraderie that my Gransha knew, a camaraderie that seems entirely natural to us but actually was hard-won by the hard work and sacrifice in tough times of the men and women of the Rhondda. It's a product of our history, our proud and challenging history, a recognition of all that lived experience we find in other people, of the common humanity we share with them. And that's the true wealth of the Rhondda. People.

9

Corona!

I'M GOING TO begin this chapter with a single word, a word you might not associate with the Rhondda: 'Corona'.

You're probably wondering now if I'm going to talk about the virus, or Mexican lager. But for people of my generation, in the Rhondda and well beyond – across Wales and all over southern England – 'Corona' means something else: pop!

Dandelion and Burdock, Cream Soda or plain Lemonade or Orangeade... whatever your favourite fizzy flavour was, a tall, sturdy glass bottle of Corona, with its big, distinctive capital C on the label – well, that was our idea of heaven.

They don't make Corona pop anymore, but once upon a time it rivalled Coca-Cola and Pepsi across much of Britain: the most successful brand ever to come from the Rhondda. If you've driven up into the valley through Porth, you'll have spotted that factory tower emblazoned with the words 'Thomas and Evans, Welsh Hills Works'. That's where Corona began, as Welsh Hills Mineral Water.

The story really starts with a boy from Pembrokeshire. William Evans was drawn to the Valleys in their Victorian heyday. Coal was King. Tens of thousands of others were moving in to be part of the boom – and they needed to be fed, so grocery businesses were booming too. William Evans was apprenticed to a grocer called William Thomas in Aberbeeg, but young Master Evans was a quick learner, and ambitious with it. He opened a shop of his own and persuaded his boss to invest – and so 'Thomas and Evans' was born. Pretty soon, he'd made enough money to buy William Thomas out of the business, but the trading name stuck: 'Thomas and Evans' it would always be.

William Evans opened another store, and another, up and down the Rhondda and across the coalfield: shop after shop. Wherever they traded, 'Thomas and Evans' became bywords for quality – and quantity! They sold so much that they even had their own railway sidings backing onto their headquarters in Porth, so that incoming foodstuffs could be loaded in bulk straight into their warehouse. Take a walk down Porth's main shopping thoroughfare, Hannah Street, and you can still see the gold letters 'T & E' built into the façade at the top of the tallest shopfront of them all, William Evans's 'main store'.

And it was there that, one day, that something bizarre happened to Evans, something that could only have happened in a place like the Rhondda was in those days. A stranger walked in claiming, in a strong American accent, to be a Medicine Man. He'd been run out of Galveston, Texas, he said – at gunpoint!

Well, Porth was a pioneering frontier town in its own right: it made *some* kind of sense for this drifter to fetch up there. The man was certainly down on his luck. Starving, in fact. So he made a deal with William Evans. In exchange for a square meal, he promised to share the secret of making "mineral water the like of which your customers will never have tasted."

And that was how William Evans began making pop. In those days of puritanical Nonconformism and widespread concern about the evils of the demon drink, a juicy non-alcoholic alternative had obvious appeal to a teetotal chapelgoer like him. And he was smart enough to see the lucrative business opportunity too!

Whether or not the recipe really did come from Texas, Welsh Hills Mineral Water had something special about it.

Everyone got a taste for it. That factory in Porth was built to cope with the demand. And when times got tough and the Depression hit the Valleys, William Evans hit upon the idea of door-to-door delivery. The pop man would pop round, just like the milkman. Even if your purse was nearly empty, it was hard to say 'no' to a treat brought to your own doorstep.

William Evans's pop was popular! All the rage. Soon it was being marketed beyond the borders of Wales. But 'Welsh Hills', it was thought, didn't have quite the right cachet to attract customers in the English Midlands. So William Evans organised a competition, challenging his staff to come up with a brand-new brand name, and offering a grand prize of £5 for the winner. The big man appointed his senior colleagues as judges, and when they chose 'Corona', William Evans smiled and said, "In which case, I will keep my £5." It was his own entry. That's businessmen for you. Canny? Shrewd? Mean?

Whatever he was, Evans made his fortune from Corona pop. He never moved out of the Rhondda, though he lived in some style for a Baptist deacon – in a mansion called Bronwydd, not far from his business empire's headquarters in Porth. At the end of his days, he gifted the surrounding parkland to the people of Porth, and his family home became council offices. Back in the 1980s, I filmed a BBC drama-documentary there telling the story of his life, turning the humdrum offices back into the Edwardian splendour of a businessman's palace by the magic of television.

And what an extraordinary life-story it was. By the 1940s, Corona was selling an astonishing *170 million* bottles of pop a year – not bad for something that originated in a chance conversation with an American quack doctor on a street in Porth. But, after the days of William Evans and his brother Frank, the company passed out of the hands of the family. It was sold to the Beecham Group in 1958 and subsequently to Britvic. Despite of one of the most memorable advertising campaigns of the 1970s – *Every bubble's passed its FIZZical!* – Corona got overtaken by trendier soft drinks, some with big bucks from across the Atlantic to lavish on their marketing. Corona stopped trading before turn of the Millennium, though you can still buy one of the company's offshoot brands, Tango, in a whole variety of flavours that I'm sure William Evans would have approved of.

It's a frustrating end to an epic story – because, as with the wealth generated by our coal, I often wonder how much more prosperous the Rhondda would be today if only we'd held on to the assets and the profits created here, by the ingenuity of people like William Evans and the hard work of his employees. There's a lesson in that for every business in Wales today.

Anyway, the next time you hear the word 'Corona', rather than something worse, you can imagine a big bottle of pop. Ah, but which flavour? For me, every time, it's got to be Dandelion and Burdock. Not because it was said to be a tonic for sufferers of anaemia, skin problems, blood disorders, even depression; but just because, as a boy, I *loved* the taste. After all, a treat's a treat – it's not about treatment!

10

Tom Jones in Nantgwyn Street

HAVE YOU EVER met Tom Jones? I did once – well, nearly. It was 1968. Tom was already a big star. 'It's Not Unusual'. 'What's New Pussycat?' And, of course, 'Green, Green Grass of Home'. Me? I was in the Top Class of Hendrecafn Junior School in Penygraig.

Back then, I used to go home to Mam for my dinner – we wouldn't have dreamt of calling it lunch. As I've said, I had a delicate appetite, and I couldn't stomach school dinners. Anyway, one dinnertime, I was dawdling along Nantgwyn Street on my way back to school, when I saw something that – to almost use Tom's phrase – *was* unusual. A big posh car – a *lim-o-sine!* – parked opposite the terraced houses, by the new bungalows.

Now, I knew who Tom Jones was. I knew – like everybody – all about his big hits. And, crucially, I even knew – *somehow, because not everyone did know this bit* – that his manager, a man called Gordon Mills, had a home in Nantgwyn, the street just below the school. I was pretty close to top of the class in mental arithmetic, and when I saw that car, it didn't take me long to put two and two together.

I sprinted up to the school as hard as I could. All my friends were playing in the yard after their dinner. Gasping, I blurted out my news to Robbie Rees:

"TOM JONES IS DOWN NANTGWYN STREET!"

Robbie told Stephen Snook, Stephen told Gaynor Bowen, Gaynor told Delun Fox, and that was that. Suddenly, *everyone* knew! *Everyone* was crowding round the school gate, leaning out as far they could to peek down the hill for a glimpse of Tom.

No-one could actually spy anything from inside the yard. But the push-and-shove at the big, open double gates got so heavy that half a dozen titches toppled onto the pavement outside: *strictly forbidden* territory for anyone who stayed in school for dinner. More and more excited classmates tumbled forward. Before I knew it, before I could do anything to stop it, the whole schoolful of us were pelting down the hill together, careering round the bench at the bottom, coming to a breathless stop outside Mr Mills's.

And there we stood, stock-still: a big silent semi-circle, gawping at the front door. Waiting for something to happen. Though precisely what, none of us could imagine. Certainly, no-one was brave enough to go and knock at the door. Time passed. The distant school bell sounded the end of dinnertime. There was no sign of Tom. Perhaps he had his dinner later than we did.

"Perhaps his *man-anager* won't let him come out and play," said one of the titches.

Everyone knew we should have been back in the yard, lining up for afternoon lessons before the teachers came out to shepherd us in.

Minutes went by. Three… four… five of them. An eternity. Still no one moved. And then, round the corner – swooshing his cane, his face red with fury – came Mr Coles, the headmaster. We panicked and broke and ran as fast as our little legs would carry us, back up the hill, back into school and into class, settling bolt upright at our desks to await punishment.

Was it lines? Or detention? More likely, the sting of a smack on our outstretched palms with that cane. Do you know, half a century later, I can't really remember. And we never did find out if Tom Jones really had been down in Nantgwyn Street, planning his next big hit with his manager, while we all stood frozen like statues outside.

But I'll never forget the day we *thought* Wales's biggest star had turned up on the green, green grass of home.

11
Porth County

AFTER HENDRECAFN JUNIORS, I went on to Porth County. Secondary education. The curse of every child's life. Homework, tests, exams, reports. The fights, the boredom, the worry. The dearth of privacy. The sheer torture of it all. Detention. Bells. Smells. The falling out and the falling in. The teachers you hated. The classmates you despised. The compulsion to fit in. The desire to stand out. Pressure, pressure, pressure – from parents to excel, from peers to be normal, from yourself just to be yourself, in spite of them all. The hours, the days, the weeks, the whole terms when you were sick and tired of it, simply ached for it to be over, for the summer holidays to be here. The utter unfairness of the whole deal.

And yet who doesn't remember those schooldays with at least a sliver of fondness, if only for the friends we made and the seasons we had with them, and for the fact that we were young then and that was our time? *You don't know what you've got till it's gone*, or so they say. But it's not just in retrospect that our eyes can be opened to the worth of education. When the schools closed during the pandemic, many Rhondda parents told me that they began to appreciate for the first time what these institutions do for children – it turns out it's far more than reading, writing and arithmetic.

Our grandparents really valued education. It was The Way Out – the means of escape from the drudgery of the pits. Miners put pennies aside, built schools for their sons and daughters, and when universal secondary education became a right, the Rhondda Borough Council invested heavily in it. Not just one, but two levels of grammar school – local grammars up and down both valleys, and for those passing their Eleven Plus with the highest marks of all, there was the Rhondda County Grammar School at Porth. Porth County.

Porth County's reputation was well established by the time an ambitious but unconventional young headmaster was appointed to the Boys' School in 1961: Owen Vernon Jones. Sporting a fine Zapata moustache, he was known to one and all as 'Santos'. The legends about him were legion. He was said to have courted his wife by galloping on horseback up to her house on the steep slopes of Blaenclydach. Conventional school discipline wasn't really his thing. Maybe the maverick in him was attracted to a degree of anarchy. But Santos was certainly ahead of his time. He modernised the school's technology, pioneering the use of a Language Lab, and commandeering a whole classroom to install a mainframe computer. At the time – so his pupils boasted, with schoolboy exaggeration – there were only three such computers in the whole world: in the Kremlin, the Pentagon... and Porth County.

Santos was determined that his school was going places. But there were some places its pupils weren't going. Admissions Tutors at Oxford and Cambridge weren't minded to admit that any good thing could come out of a Welsh mining valley. Year after year, exceptional candidates with exceptional results were rejected out of hand. But Santos was mightily persistent. He stopped short of saddling up and tilting at the Dreaming Spires, but he refused to admit defeat. Once the first acceptance came, many more followed. Soon a stream, a torrent of Rhondda talent headed for Oxbridge every autumn.

Santos fostered a special link with one of the top Oxford colleges. I'm told that when that college researched its own past to mark its 500th anniversary recently, it found that in all that time, over any ten-year period, no other headmaster had secured more admissions. Eton and Harrow, Charterhouse and Winchester – all the elite, fee-paying public schools of Olde England: Porth County gave your boys one hell of a beating!

But, like Santos, Porth was a school with something of a split personality. *During* lessons, it was a crammer: the masters dictated, and the pupils filled their notebooks with the formulae and theorems that would secure outstanding grades from the Welsh Joint Education Committee. *Between* lessons, when the teachers retreated to the staff room, it could be bedlam. The first three forms were housed in a wooden structure put up as a temporary measure during the Second World War. It was known as 'The Ranch'. The Wild West had nothing on it. Outlaws – bullies – roamed the corridors and burst into classrooms. There were snacks to snaffle, dinner money to be extorted, pain to be inflicted simply for the pleasure of it.

Porth County's academic strengths were in the Sciences. It produced phenomenal physicists, champion chemists, brilliant biologists, maestros of maths. Many of them excelled, too, on the rugby pitch. There was less emphasis on the Arts. Once a year, a trio of stiff classical musicians were summoned up from Cardiff to bring us the delights of Mozart and Beethoven. The whole school was assembled and forced to listen, with no context, to music that instinct said was desperately boring and fuddy-duddy. The results were predictable. Catcalls and sniggers. Card schools got going on the back benches. Makeshift projectiles were launched. Wrestling matches broke out. In the pauses between pieces, Santos might make a show of chastising the boys with a swish of his cane. One year, it all got so bad that he felt he had to intervene just as the trio were getting into their stride, mid-movement. Their playing ground to a halt.

"This behaviour must stop," Santos scolded us. "If not, be warned..." We waited for the terrible threat. "...I Will Make Them Play The Whole Concert All Over Again. From. The. Very. Beginning." The poor musicians, clutching their instruments like shields, sat there with fixed grins, their vocation to bring music to the masses reduced to a punishment.

So for those of us who weren't sporty or scientists, it was a relief when the boys' school merged with the Girls' Grammar in 1972, in preparation for going comprehensive a year later. Porth County had always been about more than passing a rugby ball and passing exams. Now it became an even more rounded, more fully human place to learn. And I got to act, up close on stage, with some of those girls!

The coming comprehensive ethos was helpful too – recognising different kinds of achievement, different measures of success. And rightly so: a preparation for life needs to be about more than academic hothousing. But in practice, something may have been lost in the transition: the ambition to give every child not just schooling, which focuses the mind, but education, which broadens it. A true education, as those early pioneers of schools in the Rhondda knew, makes the very best in human learning and human experience accessible to all.

To be clear – I'm a sucker for nostalgia but I'm not arguing for a return to the 'good old days of grammar schools'. When Porth went comprehensive, its Oxbridge tradition withered and died. But more was gained, for more pupils, across the whole of the Rhondda, by treating everyone as though they had the right to the best that school could offer, by refusing to make anyone think they might be second best for life just because they hadn't excelled in a certain sort of test when they were 11.

All I'm saying is that I was – as we used to say – 'jammy'. Jammy to be born in the Rhondda, where education was valued. Jammy to pass the Eleven Plus. Jammy to come under the sway of Santos and his staff and their ambitions. Jammy to be gifted an education which was the match – *and more, as we've seen!* – of any that money could buy. Jammy that our time happened to be *the very time* when the boys began to meet the girls in class as well as outside of school.

For me, because poems and plays were my thing, that last piece of luck was the best of all. Because of it, I fell under the spell of someone who would never have taught me otherwise, one of the Girls' School staff: Denise Ormond, an inspirational English teacher who knew how to conjure life out of words on a page, how to spark magic on stage, how to work the alchemy that brings poetry alive in young minds.

So, despite all the agonies of school life, real and imagined, I'll always be grateful for my time in Porth County: that it was there, and that it was then.

12

Central Hall, Tonypandy

People very often ask why I, Annie Powell, a prominent member of the Communist Party, have such a regard for the Methodist Central Hall, Tonypandy. Well, the regard I have for the Central Hall is that it was built at a time when Rhondda was in a very poor state indeed – very high levels of unemployment, when our young people had to sing their songs in a strange land. And the part that Central Hall played during that period is worthy of remembrance forevermore.

'DESPERATE CRISIS IN the Rhondda'. If you read a headline like that these days, you'd have a fair guess about the story that might follow. But Rhondda has faced economic crises before. The one that Annie Powell, the former Mayor of the Rhondda, was talking about happened in the 1920s and 1930s. They called it the Depression. No jobs or unemployment benefits. Cruel hardship. Undernourished children. Thousands and thousands so desperate that they left the Rhondda for good – young people going into exile, having to 'sing their songs in a strange land', as Mrs Powell so eloquently put it.

But Rhondda people are resilient. Crises tend to bring out the best in us. The Rhondda's response to the Depression was energetic, imaginative and forward-thinking. In the long run, it helped to change the world, and bring into being the welfare state and National Health Service we rely on today.

One of the most energetic and inspirational responses came from the Methodist Central Hall in Tonypandy. And it was in a BBC documentary I made about Central Hall in the 1980s that Annie Powell made the comments that open this chapter. She is often said to have been Britain's first Communist Mayor, and she regularly topped the poll for the Party in the Council elections for my home ward of Penygraig. She commanded respect far and wide, beyond her card-carrying comrades, for her willingness to 'take up the cudgels' on behalf of the people who elected her – against the intransigent bureaucracy of the welfare state, as well as the naked self-interest of private landlords and the like. She was a very Welsh communist. There were stories about her, on a visit to a high-level conference in Moscow, singing *'Hen Wlad Fy Nhadau'* for Nikita Khrushchev. As a first-time voter in the 1970s, I cast my ballot for her, and I've often wondered if I've been on an MI5 watch list ever since. Mrs Powell's journey – brought up as a Welsh Baptist, then becoming a prominent member of the Methodist Central Hall before joining the Communists – is a remarkable one. Just as remarkable is the fact that, despite her Party allegiance, she was willing to broadcast such fulsome public praise for a religious institution. But, when you consider the facts, how could she do otherwise?

To people of my generation and older, Central Hall was the most distinctive landmark in the whole of Tonypandy. It dominated the crossroads just along from the Plaza cinema, at the bottom of Trinity Hill, where 'Pandy's only traffic lights stood. Central Hall boasted a commanding clocktower, and facades of white Portland stone and red brick. It looked so different to the dozens of other Nonconformist chapels up and down the valley: more like a social centre than a place of worship. And, in fact, it was both. Its main meeting space could seat a thousand people. There was a lesser hall and a warren of classrooms, games rooms, libraries and workshops spread over floor after floor. The huge building arched over the lane behind it. And every square foot was put to good use.

In the Depression, Central Hall clothed the poor, and it fed the hungry in its community kitchen. In its workshops, the unemployed themselves made toys for destitute children. It was the cultural centre of the community too, with its concerts and plays and high-class recitals. There was table tennis and darts and billiards, outdoor sports too, and summer camps for young people – all of this a good decade before the rest of the country began to take the youth club movement seriously.

In its Mock Parliament, Central Hall was a forum for debating the burning issues of the day. The resolutions it passed were prophetic – on the death penalty, on unemployment and the dreaded Means Test, on the lack of a proper health service at a time when people couldn't afford to go to hospital or even see the doctor. These things we take for granted now had to be fought for back then. Central Hall equipped a whole generation of bright Rhondda people, Annie Powell amongst them, to fight that fight. A succession of brilliant ministers there proclaimed a social gospel, one that said you shouldn't – you couldn't – divorce religion from what was going in the wider society, that no-one should be left in need while others had more than enough. And at a time of huge inequalities, that meant engaging in politics.

'The differences of humanity go deep,' wrote one of those ministers, R J Barker. 'They are not the differences of those who accept the same principles. They are differences of principle, between those who accept the values of a competitive system, and those who accept the values of a communal one.'

What would those who preached that message, the stalwarts of Central Hall, make of the world we've built, I wonder? A world where individuals can be worth billions, and companies tens of billions, and pay next to no tax at all, whilst millions of people struggle to make ends meet. I think they'd say it was obscene, and that we'd settled for a system that was even more extreme in its inequalities than the one they knew.

So when I turn the corner at the bottom of Tylacelyn Road these days, I see a big gap in front of me. The gap where Central Hall once stood. Because in changing times, with shrinking church membership, the upkeep for that massive building proved too much. It was demolished in the 1980s. To make way for a supermarket.

Is that progress? Whatever it is, I'm sorry we let it happen, because of all that Central Hall meant. Buildings are important, and buildings where people can get together to think and plan and get a grip on the world, as well as entertain themselves – well, they're precious. That's why it's great to see the use that's being made nowadays of another venerable place of worship, just up the road in Penygraig – Soar Chapel, where my mother was baptised. The brilliant charity Valleys Kids has adapted it to meet the needs of our youngsters and to feed the imagination of the community. It buzzes with energy and creativity, young lives starting to build their own futures.

Annie Powell was right to say Central Hall should be remembered forevermore. Not because it stood as a Rhondda landmark – though it did – but because of all it stood for. The bricks and mortar may have been scattered. The values they housed remain.

13

Phoning Home

DO YOU STILL have a landline? And do you still use it? Everyone's on their mobiles nowadays, aren't they? And if you *do* have a landline, all you get is nuisance calls.

When I was growing up, you were lucky if you had a phone at all. Even if you could afford one, there was a shortage of lines in the Rhondda – *not enough equipment, or not enough Post Office engineers, or...* whatever the excuse was, there was a huge waiting list, and it didn't shift for years. So if we needed to phone someone, we had to use a kiosk, and they stank of... well, they stank. Then it was 'Press Button A' and 'Press Button B' and forcing your coppers into the slot. Some boys I knew – naughty boys – didn't have to pay. They knew how to *tap* a phone, lifting the receiver and tapping quickly on the little cradle it rested on the requisite number of times for each digit of the phone number they wanted. And then they got through for free!

My Nana and Gransha lived down in Holborn Terrace with my Auntie Marion and her family. Eventually, they managed to get a phone installed. It was a *party* line, shared with the house next door. If you picked it up, you might find yourself listening to your neighbour's phone call. Or they could be listening to yours. No wonder Rhondda gossip spread so quickly.

My grandparents were given a brand new four-digit Tonypandy phone number. Unfortunately, it was very similar to the number of a club on Court Street, the Mid-Rhondda

Working Men's Club and Institute. That was its official name, anyway. But – perhaps because there was a time when they actually did keep a primate in a cage above the bar – everyone called it *The Monkey Club*. So almost every time the phone rang in Holborn Terrace, and Auntie Marion picked it up, the voice on the other end would say, "'Ullo, is that The Monkey Club?" It drove them nuts!

Is that the Monkey Club? The phrase stuck in our family – for decades. In my Auntie Marion's final years, she had an intercom fitted so she didn't have to struggle to the front door to let visitors in. Whenever I went there, I used to press the buzzer and say mischievously, "'Ullo, is that The Monkey Club?" And *sometimes*, before she twigged on that it was me, she would answer indignantly, "No, this is Tonypandy..." and give out her old number.

We had to wait for much longer than my grandparents in Holborn Terrace to get a phone in our house, and when we did, it wasn't a Tonypandy number. The GPO must have run out of those. So we had a *Brynmeurig* number: Brynmeurig 479. Just three digits, but 'Brynmeurig' sounded posh and rather exclusive to me. I took to answering the phone by declaiming 'Bryn-MAY-rig Fwah Sevin Neinah' in a swanky voice. It was weeks before a friend told me the truth about 'Brynmeurig'. It was actually a rusty old GPO van parked on the hill behind the Post Office in 'Pandy with a temporary exchange lashed up inside.

Now that we had a phone, though, I could use it! I could call up *girls*. And chat them up, like they did in the movies. Our phone – like everyone else's I knew in the Rhondda – was fixed to the wall in the passage at the bottom of the stairs, like it was in the hall of some grand residence where the butler would answer it. Some chance! It was freezing out there in the winter but at least it gave me a bit of privacy. I'd sit there for hours plucking up the courage to phone one of the two girls from school I had my eye on. I'll call them Sue and Jean, because... well, because they were called Sue and Jean. The problem was that Sue and Jean spent all day in school talking to each other, not me. Despite that, when we all went home, the first thing they did was phone *each other* for another little chat – a chat that went on and on... and on. What one earth could they have left to say to each other? They'd been sitting next to each other all day long! I sat there shivering in the gloom of the passage, trying and trying and trying to get through. But every time I rang either of them in the hope of starting a courtship, the insistent, repeated beeping tone told me bluntly that – in a manner of speaking – they were already engaged.

The first time I used a phone at work was when I was a student in a summer job in Cardiff. Every desk in the office had a phone. More lines than half of Mid-Rhondda. And there was a switchboard to take incoming calls. On my first morning, the very first thing the boss did was to give me a phone number to call and a message to pass on. Nervously, I dialled the number. Literally dialled, of course – on one of those plastic dials with a hole for each number which you had to put your forefinger in and wind around. The number I was given was long, an area code and all. I was so nervous my index finger slipped the first three times. Even when I did manage to dial the whole number properly, I got nothing. Just a dead line. All fingers and thumbs, I must have tried fifty times before I gave up and went to confess to the boss that I'd failed miserably. "Can't get through!?" he fumed. Then the penny dropped, and he smiled. "Did you dial 9 for an outside line first?"

Later that summer I went to visit a college friend in the far west of Ireland. The family had a fantastic house – wonderful sea views and lawns that went down to the cliff edge. But they wouldn't mind me saying that, in telecommunications terms, they lived in a place that – even for a Rhondda boy of that era – was a step back in time. They did have a phone, but the handset looked to me suspiciously like the wind-up one in *Dr Finlay's Casebook*. And their phone number was Milltown Malbay 19. Just *two* digits. Now, being a good boy, I wanted to call home to tell Mam that I'd arrived safely. To call long distance or internationally, I was told, you had to speak to the operator in the local exchange. As soon as I put my ear to the receiver, I heard a woman's voice say, "Did you get that leak fixed? And how are the daughters? I saw you up in town yesterday. That new dress of yours fits well..."

"I'm sorry," I said, rather alarmed. "I wanted the operator."

"I *am* the operator."

"Oh... *good*. I'd like to place a call, then, please. To Wales. The number's Brynmeurig..."

"*Well, now...* Who the hell are you? And why the hell would you be wanting to call Wales?"

That was a life lesson for me: the Rhondda wasn't the only place where people took a neighbourly interest in other people's phone calls.

14

On a Rhondda Bus

WHAT WAS YOUR favourite toy when you were small? Have a think. I'll tell you about mine now in a minute.

When I was a boy it was the *normal* thing for Rhondda children to go out and play. With no adult supervision, of course. *That* would have been unimaginable. Every child, no matter how tiny, played outside: in the muddy *gwlis* and lanes, on spoil tips and filthy waste ground and derelict colliery workings on the verge of collapse. It was natural. It was healthy. Free of interfering grown-ups, in our own big world – an eighth of a mile from side to side – we'd play marbles, bolter, strong horses, and, right in the middle of the street, soccer, touch rugby or cricket. Sometimes we'd bring our favourite toys out with us. The boys would have cap guns, robots, Dinky cars and vans; girls had roller skates, skipping elastics and dolls – some of them, like Chatty Cathy, could even talk!

I was always a bit shy, however, about bringing out my favourite toy. I knew I'd get teased about it. It was something I should really have grown out of when I was much younger. I'd have been two or three when I first got it, I suppose. But I kept it for years and years, long after my friends had thrown away whatever had amused them at that age. But why would I get rid of it? It could take me anywhere! And I was devoted to it. There's scarcely a photograph of me as a boy without it.

It was my lovely sky-blue steering wheel.

The steering wheel had a white gearstick attached, and a squishy red disc at its centre, a disc you could push to sound a squeaky horn (at least until the air bag inside got tragically punctured one day). But best of all was the vertical column that the hub of the wheel sat on, a column that had a black rubber suction pad at its base.

Using that suction pad, if you sat on the front seat at the top of a double-decker bus, you could attach the steering wheel to the body of the vehicle and you could drive the bus *all the way to Blaencwm or Blaenrhondda!* And not just to the top of the valley. Up to Clydach, down to Porth, Trebanog, Tonyrefail, all the way up the Rhondda Fach to Maerdy. Any route you could think of, on the whole Rhondda Transport network.

We didn't have a car, so Rhondda buses featured large in my young life. Mam or Nan or Nana, whoever was taking me out, could be sure that my blue steering wheel would be coming too. They knew where we'd have to sit: front seat, top deck. As soon as we'd sat down, I'd start driving the bus, unfailing in my concentration on the road, taking seriously my duty of care for the safety of all aboard. There was a little ditty some of my classmates used to sing back then – *'Oh, you'll never get to heaven on a Rhondda bus, 'cos a Rhondda bus makes too much fuss.'* That didn't make any sense to me. The upper deck of a Rhondda bus was as close to heaven as I could possibly imagine.

So that I could keep strictly to the timetable, and make my conductor's work easy, I learned by heart the exact locations and the names of all the bus stops: *The Naval Colliery, 'Pandy Lights, Partridge Square, Old Tyntyla, The Star, Carter's Corner...*

Once I was old enough to put pen to paper, I'd sit on the floor at home with my marvellous toy by my side, drawing up detailed timetables of my own, inventing routes to Charlie's sweet shop or Hendrecafn School or Auntie Bet's house, routes down the side-streets, lanes and *gwlis* of Penygraig and Tonypandy, shortcuts inaccessible to Rhondda Transport, but massively convenient for me and my family, where my magic steering wheel would come into its own.

There was one real bus route that was truly magical for me, although single-deckers ran on it, which made it tricky for me to get a seat with my steering wheel which had a proper view of the road ahead. It was the summer service to Porthcawl, operated jointly by Rhondda Transport and Red & White.

From distant Aberdare, the bus came over the mountain to Maerdy, down the Rhondda Fach to Tylorstown, up and over to the Rhondda Fawr via Penrhys, and down through Tonypandy, before picking us up – not at the Naval Colliery, where all the valley buses would allow boarders by request, but only at the stop by Jones the Fruiterer's opposite The Adare, a hundred yards down the road at the bottom of the hill. This route was special! And there was a circular tour of Gilfach Goch, Garden Village and Evanstown thrown in.

The final destination, an hour and a half distant, would have been the star attraction for any other child: Porthcawl's golden seaside and all the fun of the Fair. I liked them well enough, it's true, but for me the real thrill was... Bridgend Bus Station.

Arriving there, I had to steer my bus past a long row of others that were already parked up and come to a precise stop, nose-in to the stand. Then, after a five-minute break, it was time to leave for the last leg to the coast and – *oh, my goodness!* – I had to *reverse* away from the stand, avoiding pedestrians and all the other traffic. I never failed to execute this complex manoeuvre perfectly, even on the way back home, however drowsy I was from a day on the sands of Coney Beach, with a tummy full of toffee apple and doughnuts.

Eventually, inevitably, came the *Toy Story* moment: the day when I told my parents soberly that I was too old for a steering wheel, and that they should give it away. A week later, I was so miserable, missing it so much, that I had to beg for its return. I was 34 at the time.

No, no, I was joking about my age. But not about getting the steering wheel back. Whether Dad had wisely kept the original hidden away, or Mam indulgently had to go out and buy a new one – well, I was so familiar with my beloved toy that I must have been able to tell at the time, but by now I've forgotten which. The only thing that mattered was that I had it in my hands again. But from then on it was a secret pleasure, one I never ever talked about while playing out in the back lane or up in Hughes Street beyond.

One final story. My love of buses, and my bond with that steering wheel, led me to be dismissive of all other forms of transport. On one famous occasion, my uncle got the worst of that. Uncle Robert was an exotic figure to me. *He lived in Hawthorn! He had a moustache! He had a motor car!* One day, he turned up to give Mam and me a lift to Cardiff. Naturally I was disappointed not to be going by bus, but Uncle Robert was in the habit of pressing half-a-crown into my palm whenever he visited, a gift of astonishing generosity. Offered the novelty of a car journey to the capital, I sensed that it was in my pecuniary interests to go along for the ride, as it were.

Sadly, as the trip progressed, it became evident that my faith had been badly misplaced. My uncle was in possession of a severely deficient sense of direction. Instead of following the proper route into Talbot Green, he skirted around the edge of the town, missing out the bus station altogether. A few miles further on at Pontyclun, he ignored the main shopping thoroughfare, scooting down an unfamiliar side road that I could only hope led onwards towards Miskin. And when we got *there*, my uncle wilfully ignored the turn that led to the Miskin Arms, the centre of village life and *a really important bus stop*. Instead, he carried on along a strange road which was wider and possibly more direct, but clearly *just the wrong way*. It was the last straw. "Uncle Robert," I said, turning in the passenger seat to admonish the wayward driver, speaking his name slowly and sternly, as I'd noted that grown-ups tended to do when it was necessary to offer mature guidance to an errant child, "You do go an *awful* funny way to Cardiff!"

15

Dai Chips: A Rhondda Time Lord

DAI CHIPS. IF you went to Porth County in the 1960s or 1970s, or Tonypandy Grammar in its last years, or Tonypandy Comprehensive School early on, you'll know who I'm talking about. Mr David Thomas, head of History at Porth, later the Headmaster of 'Pandy Grammar and Deputy Head of the Comp.

Dai Chips was a real Rhondda character: witty, passionate, unconventional. History's Most Eccentric History Teacher. He swore blind that he was a Time Lord and claimed that the clapped-out Morris Minor he drove was his Tardis. He was a short man – very short: no taller than the titches of Form One. Dapper, always neatly turned out in jacket and tie, and his specs with trademark half-rim frames. He'd arrive at school and struggle away from his time machine, if that's what it was, lugging a large briefcase in one hand. The briefcase would be packed with weighty reference books, and scores of exercise books he'd taken home for marking. My great friend Phil George, who was also taught by him, always pictures him leaning dramatically to one side as he walked, to counterbalance the massive load he was carrying.

Dai Chips was a strict disciplinarian. Perhaps because he was noticeably shorter than almost everyone he taught, he kept order with flashes of volcanic temper. In an era when schoolmasters regularly dispensed physical punishment, he'd frighten us back into line by threatening to yank our hair: 'Side-head Tweaks', a sudden twist of our sideburns, for minor misdemeanours; and 'Excruciatingly Painful Top-head Extractions' for anything more serious. If he ever had to tell the whole class off, he declaimed angrily and apparently in all seriousness that he'd turn us into toads and tie us to his windscreen wipers. No-one really believed him, though on the last day of term one summer, some schoolboy prankster knotted a dozen plastic toy frogs to the wipers of his Morris Minor. Every pupil who walked past shivered with a moment's doubt – were Dai Chips's supernatural powers real after all?

David Hywel Thomas had been born in Cwmparc in 1935. His mother was a nurse; his father had left school aged 12 to go underground. They were strong socialists and Welsh Methodists – two things that influenced Dai Chips for the rest of his life. He got his nickname as a schoolboy at Porth County: he would climb over the school wall to go and get his lunch from the local chip shop. He was bright. He got a first-class degree in History from Cardiff and trained to be a teacher at Cambridge. His teaching practice was done at Eton – imagine if he'd stayed on there, getting to grips with all those future prime ministers! British politics would be quite different by now.

Instead, he got his first teaching post at the King Edward VII Academy in Kings Lynn, where he was soon famous for snorting snuff in class – another of his idiosyncrasies – and challenging his pupils to take a pinch themselves. But the pull of the Rhondda was strong. In 1961, he came back to head the History Department at Porth County, bringing his own unique teaching methods with him.

Dai Chips was a Dictator. A Great Dictator, but a dictator nonetheless. In the days before much of Welsh history was properly covered in print, and without today's instant online access to source material, Dai Chips spent 95% of every lesson dictating to us, at breakneck speed, whole chapters of his own research work and theses. We had to write it all out word for word, page after page, directly into our exercise books. The only respite we got was if a sentence began with the word 'However', when – each and every time – Dai Chips would pause to deliver, melodramatically, a deafening instruction about punctuation. It came across like an overstated parody of a fairground barker: "HowevAHHH, CommAHHHHHH..." and then, after a long pause, and in the most reasonable of tones, as though nothing out of the ordinary had just occurred, "...always a comma after 'However'." Then, instantly, the pace of his dictation shot up to full throttle again, and on we went.

Dai Chips's teaching method was further complicated by dividing the material into a rigid hierarchy of topics, sections, subsections and sub-subsections, like some complex legal contract. Each heading was cross-referenced to a detailed analysis of past exam papers, offering model answers to any question the WJEC might throw at us. It was convoluted. It was instruction by rote. According to all that modern psychology tells us about the ways we learn, it was surely a guarantee of academic underachievement. However, *(always a comma after 'However'!)* it turned out to be amazingly effective. At the end of Form Four, a year early, the 33 boys in our class sat History O level. We all passed. Something like 28 of us got top marks, a Grade 1. An astounding performance: I think it even merited a mention in the *Rhondda Leader*.

In one lesson, we were onto one of Dai Chips's 'banker topics', as he called them – things we were bound to get an exam question about: the history of the South Wales Coalfield. Dai Chips was dictating a subsection, or perhaps a sub-subsection, analysing the strategies of the coal barons, and the rise of entrepreneurship. The bell was about to go for dinnertime. We were all flagging, but Dai Chips powered on with his dictation: "In 1828, Robert Thomas opened an exceptionally productive pit at Abercanaid, near Merthyr, but he died five years later. However, (*always a comma...*, etc.) when his widow Lucy took over the business, she hit upon the idea of selling the coal..."

Dai Chips left the briefest of pauses at that precise point, and an image flashed into our heads of these poor miners, labouring away for years and years digging up all that coal, a huge mountain of the stuff just sitting there at the top of the pit, with no-one having cottoned on to the idea that you could sell it. One of the boys laughed. And laughter – especially in a classroom – is contagious. In a flash, we were all giggling uncontrollably. Dai Chips started laughing too. Of course, *he* knew that the full sentence read, "...she hit upon the idea of selling the coal *further afield in the lucrative London market*." But we never got that far. Thankfully, Dai Chips had seen the funny side himself, so we didn't get turned into toads either.

When he retired from teaching, Dai Chips was ordained as a Methodist minister, taking charge of the chapel he'd been brought up in, Capel y Parc in Cwmparc. He was much in demand, locally and *further afield*. The weekend before he died in 2010, he'd preached at two Welsh chapels in London. His widow Barbara – also a much-loved teacher – remained in their family home in Tonypandy until she passed away in 2022. But Dai Chips's legacy lives on in the generations of schoolchildren he influenced and inspired. He was one of the pioneers of the idea that Rhondda children ought to study Rhondda history. That lesson about the coal industry was typical. Academic study of the coalfield's past was still in its infancy then. Most of the material Dai Chips fed us wasn't available in any textbook. He'd gathered and organised it all himself. And he insisted on squeezing as much local history as possible onto a syllabus which, even under the *Welsh* Joint Education Committee, was dominated by English kings and European wars.

To end on a personal note, it's because Dai Chips taught us that history begins at home that Phil George and I, as television producers in later life, gave so much emphasis to *place* when we made *The Story of Wales*, the BBC's 'official' history of our nation, in 2012. If the series is back on the BBC iPlayer (it still crops up there from time to time), check it out, and you'll see what I mean. Time and again, the audience's delighted reaction to stories located in their own home patch was *I never knew that!* Unlike us, not everyone in Wales had had the privilege of being taught by Dai Chips, or anyone like him (not that anyone was like him). As the actor Michael Sheen put it, "*The Story of Wales* gave me the education I wish I could have got in school." Learning from Dai Chips *was* an education. It was massive fun, too.

16

Treorchy's Rugby Dream

WHAT DO YOU dream about these days? The things we imagine when we're asleep are often bizarre, though they reveal a lot about our deepest hopes and fears... *or so they say!*

A dream can also be something that we hold onto when we're wide awake – a cherished desire or a grand ambition. TV talent shows are full of wannabe singers who talk about 'living the dream'. But there's another sort of dream that's more characteristic of the Rhondda, I'd say, and truer to our history – a dream that isn't just about personal ambition, about chasing fame and fortune for ourselves: it's a kind of vision that includes others, that aims to do something to better all our lives.

It's almost 30 years since the BBC made the TV series *The Dream* about Treorchy Rugby Club's amazing rise to the top. It's a story that's been told many times – there's a reason for that, which we'll come to – but it's worth telling again, because there are parts of it... well, if you didn't remind yourself that it actually happened in real life, you'd swear that somebody had dreamt it up.

Treorchy's rugby Dream came to fruition in the 1990s. But the story begins, I suppose, 20 years before that: with a group of boys who were at school with me in the early 1970s – *duw, duw,* it's *fifty* years ago! As I've explained, Porth County was known as a rugby school. In that Golden Era for

Welsh rugby, 'County' would take on the best in the land. There were fleet-footed backs like my classmates Michael Chapman, Julian Roberts, David Latcham and Stephen Snook, but the 'grunt' came from the forwards – a bunch of real tough nuts! Our 'Terrible Eight' included characters like Adrian Owen: flame haired, and with a temper to match the cliché; Phil Davies: a monster of a prop; and Chris Jones: a flanker-cum-hooker who, in terms of brutality, was in another league altogether.

These were all intelligent boys, that wasn't in dispute. They'd passed with top marks in their Eleven Plus to get into Porth County. But something happened to them when they took the field of play. And when they left school and formed the core of the Treorchy club side, there was *big* trouble. There were brawls and battles, sly punches, stampings and sendings-off. For a while, Treorchy became a byword for rugby thuggery. When the elite players of Cardiff had to come and play a Cup match at Treorchy's Oval, those capital-city slickers donned their kits trembling in fear of their lives. The noises off from the home changing room weren't exactly a welcome to the hillsides. And sure enough, once the game kicked off, so did the slugfest.

Season after season, things went on that you couldn't make up. Chris Jones was banned for life – *twice*. Somehow, he continued to play... and fight. He used to turn up for matches with an axe in his kit bag. Then something even more extraordinary happened. Chris found God. In a police cell in Brecon. Drunk, he'd been arrested for affray at the Jazz Festival.

Now, whatever your take might be on the belief he found that night, there's no doubt that it transformed his behaviour, his character and the course of his life, all for the better. Meanwhile, Phil Davies, his old Porth County teammate, had spent time away from the Rhondda and was a convert to another powerful agent of change: marketing.

Marketing wasn't such a well-developed business tool back then. It was pretty much unheard of in rugby circles. The game was still amateur – at least in the way it was administered. But these Treorchy boys saw that change was coming. And they saw a way to steal a march on the fusty old traditional clubs like Cardiff, Swansea and Llanelli, who'd dominated the Welsh game for decades. Treorchy, in their Grand Plan, would rise up the leagues, and up again, taking their place at the very top table of Welsh club rugby. And more than that, the club would become one of a small number of elite teams playing against the best in Europe, in the new professional competitions that Phil Davies had the vision to see coming. The Dream was about to become a reality.

While all this was going on, I was working my way up the ladder at BBC Wales. There was a new fashion for documentaries about real life, for ordinary, extraordinary things that the camera could film as they were happening: *docusoaps*, they were called. I realised what a great docusoap it would make if we could be in the Treorchy dressing room as they finally made it to the top. With my colleague Phil George – another Treorchy boy who'd been to Porth County – I headed up to the club to see if they'd be willing to give our film crews access. We were met with open arms. Publicity, you see, was a key part of marketing.

There was something special about the series that came about as a result. In the years that followed, I was involved in producing lots of rugby documentaries, many of them award-winners: the story of the triumphant Lions Tour of 1971; a reconstruction of the famous Wales vs. New Zealand game of 1905; profiles of Barry John and of the Llanelli team who beat the All Blacks; a fly-on-the-wall series about the modern-day Scarlets. All these programmes were directed by people who knew their rugby. But for Treorchy's rugby *Dream*, the director was Eric Styles, someone who knew next to nothing about the game. Eric Styles. He was well-named.

He *was* stylish – a Valleys boy fresh out of Film School when I gave him his break into broadcasting – but he was more of a drama director, really. I saw his name just the other day, the final credit on *The Pact*, a big drama series from the BBC.

Back then, he was chosen for the Treorchy series precisely because we wanted to appeal to viewers well beyond the core rugby audience. And we wanted to do that because the Dream dreamed by Phil Davies, Chris Jones, his brother Clive, the late Neil Hutchings (the inspirational club chairman), and all the other leading lights of Treorchy RFC, the Dream they were making happen – and it did all come true, just as they'd foreseen – that Dream was about more than rugby. It was about giving hope to a whole community. About helping young men, in particular, to see that there was more to life than drink and drugs. About showing the Rhondda that it could achieve great things if it pulled together with imagination, with insight into the way the world works, and with the kind of intelligence that has always marked our valley out, just as distinctively as the physical strength of our rugby forwards and our colliery faceworkers.

Idris Davies – the working-class poet of the South Wales Coalfield who knew the Rhondda well – wrote of 'a dreamer in the mining town' who wandered in the evening to the hills:

> There in the dusk the dreamer dreamed
> Of shining lands, and love unhampered
> By the callous economics of a world
> Whose god is Mammon.

Treorchy's Rugby Dream faded fast when the big clubs cottoned on to the marketing techniques that had been pioneered in the Rhondda. 'Callous economics' had its way. But there was something beautiful about that Dream all the same, something powerful which was heard 'among the far undying echoes of the world', as Idris Davies puts it later in his poem. Something that said – and still says – that the Rhondda has vision, has talent, has the acumen and the gumption not just to take its place amongst the very best, but to lead the way.

It was all a long time ago now. I wonder if any of us have a Dream like that, in whatever aspect of life, for the Rhondda in the 2020s.

17
Why It's THE Rhondda

JOHN ON THE RHONDDA – I'm fond of it as a title for my radio talks and podcasts. The triple rhyme, J*ohn on* the Rh*on*dda, is catchy. Someone told me the other day that it's a perfect of piece of *cynghanedd*, that strict form of Welsh poetry that wins chairs at the National Eisteddfod. Well, I say *'someone* told me', but if you'll forgive a small piece of bardic one-upmanship, it wasn't just anyone: it was a former Archdruid of Wales, a double winner of the Eisteddfod Crown and Chair! So I'd say he knows what he's talking about.

But how come it's called *John on THE Rhondda*? Why *'the* Rhondda'? Some people insist that we should call our valley simply 'Rhondda', not *'the* Rhondda'. I disagree – and I'll tell you why, now just...

People are funny about the exact way we speak, the precise words we use. They get very aeriated about it. 'Aeriated': now there's a word in itself! Its root has got nothing to do with "'aving your *'air* off" about something, though it means the same thing. Anyway, I got *aeriated* with a friend of mine the other day. He'd written a book about football, and I wrote a little review of it online, saying how much I'd enjoyed it, even though I'm no big fan of soccer. And then *he* posted – thanking me for my kind words about his book, but stating in no uncertain terms that it was about *football*, not soccer.

You see, some people think 'soccer' is an Americanism, a word the Yanks invented because they think their version, American football, takes precedence over all the other versions of football. Well, I said, getting on my high horse, *my* use of it has got nothing to do with the United States. When I was growing up in the Rhondda, we used the words 'football' and 'soccer' interchangeably for Association Football. Yes, there was the *Football* Echo, fair enough. We bought the 'Pink 'Un' for the League results on a Saturday night. But, once we'd read them, we might easily and naturally say, "Let's have a game of soccer up Hughes Street." And once I'd gone public in saying that, it all kicked off, so to speak. Everyone piled in. And perhaps because I was attuned to the kind of silly spats that crop up over social media, I started following another row about language that was going on at the same time – one about '*the* Gower'.

'*The* Gower'? We're supposed to call it 'Gower', just 'Gower', apparently. Anything else is 'unhistorical', because 'the Gower' is short for 'the Gower Peninsula', and 'Gower' is more than the peninsula itself: it includes Swansea and Gowerton and lots of other places well inland, as any student of ancient Welsh boundaries and the Norman invasion of Wales is supposed to know. "Placing the definite article before 'Gower' is not just an unnecessary intrusion – it is disrespectful of the history of Wales," we were told.

Well, pardon me, but ever since I can remember, ever since Mam and Dad used to take me for idyllic family summer holidays to a little wooden shack on Plunch Lane above Limeslade Bay, we've always called it 'the Gower'. And what about that ditty Ryan and Ronnie used to sing, about 'Uncle Mike, who 'ad a motorbike.' Where did he ride it 'at a 'undred miles an hour'? 'Around *the* Gower'! I rest my case. In my book, it's fine to say *the Gower*, even if many locals think plain *Gower* is more correct. And, likewise, it's *the Rhondda* even if some of my teachers in Porth County tried to school us into saying just *Rhondda* instead. "I come from Rhondda" – I don't think so! "I come from the Rhondda" – *now* I'm talking tidy.

John Geraint

But why "*the* Rhondda"? There are very few place names we use when we're speaking English which have 'The' in front of them. Aside from the Gower, and off the top of my head, the only ones that spring to mind are The Bronx and The Hague. The Bronx is a famous New York borough and there's a heated debate about the origin and use of 'The' before its name. Either it comes from 'the Bronx River' or – more fancifully – from Bronck, the family name of some original Swedish settlers (people would talk about going to visit "the Broncks"). And The Hague is a literal translation of the Dutch 'Den Haag'. In languages other than English, the use of the definite article before a place name is much more common. The French have Le Havre and Le Mans and La Rochelle. And, of course, Los Angeles and Las Vegas are so familiar that we scarcely think of them any more as Spanish names beginning with a plural form of the definite article.

In Welsh too, many place names have the definite article, *Y* or *Yr* (The), in front of them. Rhyl in north Wales is Y Rhyl in Welsh. Some people think the name originally comes from the Welsh *yr* before the English 'hill' – Yr Hill, The Hill – which would be a bit odd, since as far as I know there aren't any hills in Rhyl. Another example, familiar to all of us from road signs on trips to the seaside, is Barry – Y Barri in Welsh. And here in the Rhondda, Porth is Y Porth (The Gateway). So yes, in Welsh, it's natural to say Y Rhondda, *the* Rhondda, for the whole valley. Though incidentally, in Welsh, if we want to make clear that it's a valley we're talking about, we say Cwm Rhondda, like the hymn tune, not Cwm Y Rhondda, even though Barry Island is Ynys Y Barri (The Barry Island). Language is rarely completely consistent. That's its beauty.

So I think the 'the' in *the* Rhondda must come from us imitating the Welsh Y Rhondda. But that's still not enough to explain why we've kept it in English, calling it 'the Rhondda', when we don't say 'the Porth' or 'the Barry'. My guess is that it's something to do with the fact it's a geographical feature –

a valley – not the name of a town. That would explain why we say 'the Gower': it's a peninsula, a geographical feature – even if, historically, it's been more than that. By now, it seems to me – and I bet to you too – completely natural to talk about 'the Rhondda'. *John on Rhondda* might be technically correct, and it keeps the triple rhyme, but it just sounds wrong, and rather affected in my opinion (*though one of my listeners took umbrage at me confessing that!*).

By the way, I'm a stickler for 'Rhondda' not 'Ronda', as some newsreaders from… *um*, further afield have been known to pronounce it. The 'dd' in Welsh is definitely NOT a 'd' sound! But I'm much more relaxed about the initial 'Rh' in Rhondda. I know it should be 'RH-ondda', with a proper voiceless alveolar trill, as linguists call it, believe it or not. But the exaggerated RH some Welsh speakers insist on grates on me, and it doesn't sound natural to the Rhondda accent, even in Welsh: 'the Rhondda' with a moderately rolled 'R' is fine. I'm told that's closer to the way native Glamorganshire Welsh-speakers would have pronounced it years ago anyway.

And '*the* Rhondda' it is, not just 'Rhondda' – I think we can all agree on that. Can't we?

18

Libraries Gave Us Power

ONE OF THE loudest concerts I ever filmed was in… the Library. Yes, the Library. Far from the hush normally associated with dusty reading rooms and shelf after shelf of books catalogued according to the Dewey Decimal System, this gig rocked. But it *was* in 'the Library' – that's what we called the old Miners' Institute on Llwynypia Road, Tonypandy. By the time I was filming there in the 1980s for a BBC TV show with Treorchy band Peruvian Hipsters, the building was essentially a club, popular with young people for discos and parties. But to my mind – and according to the interview I did with lead guitarist Nigel Buckland – the group played that night in the spirit of the old Miners' libraries, the Hipsters' call-and-response rock ballads echoing with a message of communal solidarity and the hope of better things to come for the youth of the valley.

The Library: I've got to think carefully about how I pronounce that word. What comes naturally to me is to say '*li-bury*', and I have to make an effort to remember that the word has *two* 'r's in it, and it's supposed to be pronounced 'lib*rary*'. But I'm pretty sure that most of the people I grew up with said '*li-bury*' – and that includes someone I know who spent a whole career as a librarian in the Rhondda, so there!

However you say it, 'Libraries gave us power'. So sang another Welsh band, Manic Street Preachers. The opening line of the Manics' signature hit 'A Design for Life' was inspired by the inscription above the entrance to the Pillgwenlly Library in Newport: 'Knowledge is Power'. The phrase conjures up the mission of the scores of Miners' Institutes right across the coalfield that put education at the heart of Welsh working-class life. These were social spaces that offered the prospect not just of individual self-improvement, but the enrichment of communal life for everyone.

The Institute libraries were the "miners' universities", or what historian Dai Smith called the "brains of the coalfield". They broadened minds, expanded horizons, fired imaginations and gave readers a glimpse of a life beyond the toil and hardship of their daily lives, a vision of a better world.

From the very start, these miners' libraries, self-funded by the colliers themselves, were so important and so valued by the people who used them that their autonomy was jealously guarded. In 1903, over in the Cynon Valley, the *Aberdare Leader* reported that the people of Penrhiwceiber had turned down an offer of £700 (the equivalent of more than £100,000 today) from the wealthy American industrialist Andrew Carnegie to help establish a public library in the area. Penrhiwceiber already had a splendid library at its Miners' Institute. The community didn't see why it should give up its independence or pay twice over for a library service in their council rates, or indeed be beholden to man whose handouts were frequently regarded as blood money. All of this was before Prime Minister David Lloyd George's determination to build a country 'fit for heroes' after the trauma of the First World War led to the 1919 Public Libraries Act. That Act made county councils responsible for providing public libraries. But such was the popularity and quality of the 21 Miners' Institute libraries in the Rhondda that it wasn't until the late 1930s, and only after long-drawn-out and often very bitter negotiations, that it was finally agreed that the Rhondda *Borough* Council should adopt the Public Library

Act. Even then, they began by using 13 of the Institutes to loan out books.

The Miners' Institute libraries were superbly well-stocked. The one in Cymmer, near Porth, had 8,000 titles. The 1903 catalogue of the Maerdy library listed books in Welsh and English on subjects ranging from law, medicine and science to poultry-keeping and folklore. 60 different magazine and newspaper titles were available too – just as well the library stayed open until 11 o'clock at night.

If you're looking for any further evidence of the huge impact the libraries made, turn to the pages of the pioneering travel writer H V Morton. Henry Morton made his name as a journalist covering the opening of Tutankhamun's Tomb. In 1932, he published his famous book *In Search of Wales*. In it, he writes...

> At a street corner in Tonypandy I heard two young miners discussing Einstein's Theory of Relativity. I know this was exceptional, but it is significant; and it is true. It will not seem out of the way to any one who knows South Wales... Smith's bookshop in Cardiff... recently delivered [a copy of the] *Oxford English Dictionary*, which cost £45, to the Workmen's Institute at Ton-yr-efail. This £45 was saved by miners in twopences! And they followed it up by saving £39 for *the Encyclopaedia Britannica*!

Travelling the length of the Rhondda during the Depression, Henry Morton calls it 'Heartbreak Valley'. But his admiration for the intellect of the working-class people he encounters grows and grows... 'I have met miners,' he writes, 'whose culture and gift of self-expression seem to me nothing short of miraculous. These men know how to think.'

One of the colliers Morton meets explains to him how it's *books* that liberate the intelligence and the imagination of men who spend all their working lives underground:

> Think what reading means to an active mind that is locked away in the dark for hours every day! Why, in Mid-Rhondda there are 40,000 books a month in circulation from four libraries...

Forty thousand books! What an amazing statistic. During those years of hunger, the appetite for reading shown by the people of 'Heartbreak Valley' is astounding.

After the Second World War, the Borough Council opened branch libraries for its 25,000 registered readers up and down the Rhondda. Thomas and Evans gifted the Lucania buildings for the Porth branch, and in 1950, Caersalem Chapel in Tonypandy was converted into a public library. It was from there that I borrowed my first books in the 1960s.

From my earliest years, I was always a keen reader, but I wonder how much more I would have appreciated the works of Enid Blyton and then Isaac Asimov, Agatha Christie and J R R Tolkien on the shelves of Tonypandy Library had I known what a proud tradition of respect for reading those shelves represented. The books I borrowed were free of charge – so long as I remembered to return them in time. Did that make them less valuable in my eyes? *You don't know what you've got till it's gone,* as I've mentioned before – so let's hope that we learn to cherish and protect our public libraries as well as our other public services before they're taken away from us.

As the mines shut, so did the Miners' Institutes – or they became just social clubs like the one where I filmed the Hipsters' gig. Now it's the South Wales Miners' Library in Swansea which houses the printed books and pamphlets of more than 60 Institutes and Welfare Halls from across the coalfield. The Miners' Library also has sound recordings, videos and posters, and a wonderful collection of the banners of the Miners' Lodges. It's an educational resource in the best traditions of the old Miners' Institutes – I've drawn many times on its expertise and its treasures for the documentaries I've made about our shared history. Because of what it represents as much as what it is, it should engage us and excite us just as much as the loudest, most thrilling concert we've ever had the privilege to attend, no matter where that was.

I'd like to say diolch o galon *to Hywel Matthews of Treorchy Library, who couldn't have been more helpful in searching out some of the material I've used in this chapter.*

19

The Promised Land

It was a slow day, as Paul Simon might have said. A lazy Saturday afternoon, one of those bright autumn days that might just be the last truly balmy day of the turning year. The sun was... well, not beating down exactly, but the sky was blue and it was warm enough to go shirt-sleeved. Yes, a day for Porthcawl or Southerndown, or Barry Island perhaps. And if not there, a jaunt over the Rhigos, the Bannau Brycheiniog (Brecon Beacons) brilliant in the slanting sunlight. Even a walk up the mountain here at home would have done, up the shining slopes of Carncelyn or Craig-yr-Eos.

But no... something drew me back to somewhere few people other than me, I suppose, would ever think of as the right place to while away a precious afternoon like this; somewhere no sensible person would dream of as a destination for a day-trip. I found myself on Tylacelyn, on the very road where I grew up, in the middle of Penygraig, window-shopping in those retail outlets that were still in business, with a strange bittersweet feeling in my guts, an aching for something, something to do with this place and all it means to me. What was that feeling? It has a name, a Welsh name... ah, yes... *hiraeth*. But this was a peculiar sort of *hiraeth*.

Hiraeth – you can't translate it, or so they say. Let me try. It's a kind of yearning for a person, a place or a time that you can't get back to, 'a longing to be where your spirit lives'. But perhaps because my sentimental stroll began at the top of

Tylacelyn hill, across the road from Pisgah Chapel, the kind of *hiraeth* I was feeling was pointed in a different direction.

Pisgah the chapel, you see, took its name from Pisgah the mountain: the mountain in the Bible where Moses was shown a prospect of the Promised Land. He could see it right there, in the distance, though he never got to tread the hallowed ground himself. This Pisgah – Pisgah Chapel – had a fine view of Mid-Rhondda, my Promised Land. The terraced houses drew my eye down the steep rise, towards Tonypandy; Trealaw Road in the distance slanting upwards again, up the valley towards the wooded slopes of Tyntyla; and on the left, looking down on it all, the crags of Glyncornel, prosaically topped by a TV relay mast. I stood there opposite Pisgah, gazing up at the huge stone frontage of the chapel, wondering about Moses and what he must have been feeling on his Pisgah: a yearning for the Promised Land – a kind of *hiraeth*, but a *hiraeth* directed towards what was yet to come, towards a better future, for his people if not for himself.

Pisgah. I passed by on the other side, walking on towards the few shops that were left in what was once the bustling heart of Penygraig, my hometown.

The old post office has long been closed. It's been converted into a house now, a house with a name on a plaque at the door. It's called… 'The Old Post Office'. There's a strange comfort in that. It's not just me who remembers.

A few doors along, on the corner of Hendrecafn Road, where my teenage friend John Newman once had a photography studio, there's now what anyone can instantly recognise from the shopfront as a very, very stylish hairdresser's. Nicholas James. The decor, the design, the whole set-up just oozes class. A celebrity hairstylist right here in the heart of the Rhondda! Nicholas James is from Clydach Vale, though he's worked in much more glamorous locations, and he does count celebrities on his list of clients. But – as befits any good hairstylist – he hasn't forgotten his roots. "I wanted," he's quoted as saying, "to bring back something vibrant, classy and luxurious to the Valleys. People deserve to have that here." Amen to that.

Sadly, my male-pattern baldness has reached a stage where I don't need a haircut, so I walk on. Towards something from a different era. An Aladdin's cave of a shop, its counters, drawers and shelves crammed to bursting with anything and everything you could need for those fiddly jobs around the house: Jones the Ironmongers, established 1898. It's often said to be the oldest shop in the whole Rhondda, but I knew from my childhood days that the name is misleading...

When I was a boy, we lived with my Grampa. He was long retired from a lifetime as a colliery blacksmith, but he still loved pottering about in the coalhouse up the back garden. He'd whistle away to himself, dressed in his blue dungarees, hammer or screwdriver in hand: DIY, mending things, making things. Occasionally, he'd send me 'up the road' to fetch some hardware he needed – hinges, hooks or wire, blacksmith nails, paint or polish: "Just run up *to Arthur Hopkin's* for me, *boi bach*. Tell him it's for Tommy John."

Arthur Hopkin: he'd taken over the ironmonger's, probably as long ago as during the Second World War. It's still in his family, though it continues to trade under the original name of Thomas Jones & Sons Ltd. But many Penygraig people still call it Arthur Hopkin's. And it's still got everything Tommy John could have needed – and his modern equivalent too.

Just yards away, there's another real Valleys institution, one I've mentioned in a previous chapter. Mr Creemy's. Ice cream to die for. Double Belgian Chocolate, Succulent Strawberry, Peanut Butter Overload. There's no way I'm going to get through a sunny afternoon like this without a cornet containing at least two of those exotic flavours. But I need something more substantial in my stomach first. So it's down the slope to Taylor's. They've won awards too. For fish and chips.

Taylor's is the new kid on this block – it was only established in 2004, but already it's hard to imagine Penygraig without it. And a tray of luscious chips is just the thing to keep me going. I tuck in, bold as brass in the afternoon sun, standing on the pavement outside Soar. The chapel where my mother was baptised has now been adapted – and magnificently so – by Valleys Kids. It buzzes with activity, a hub where children of all ages experience a whole range of arts and crafts that expand their skills and their imaginations. The converted building still bears the chapel name, another Nonconformist borrowing from the Scriptures. The biblical Zoar was a city of refuge, but its Welsh spelling on the frontage here – S-o-a-r – is often mistaken, understandably, to mean that this place is a refuge where young people can *soar* up high to new levels of aspiration and attainment... and have lots of fun whilst they do so.

That was it. That was my afternoon walk, from one old chapel to another. And, in between, four shops that chimed with my mood, just four amongst all the others in Penygraig that were still trading, or were now shut up. A classy hairdresser's, a classic ironmonger's, award-winning ice cream, champion chips. It wouldn't take much – just another quartet of businesses with similar standards, similar ambitions, perhaps – and Penygraig as a place to come and shop would... well, *soar* up to a different plane, set on a path towards being something really special, something we can all be proud of. They've done it in Treorchy, with their Best of British title-winning high street. Why not here, too?

And that, I realise, was the *hiraeth* I was feeling – a *hiraeth* not solely for the past, although there were many reminiscences caught up in it. But a *hiraeth* for what might yet be. A yearning for a Promised Land, somewhere tantalisingly within reach, if only we could realise it.

20

Gateway to the Stars

I'M A SUCKER for space travel. Oh, I know there are better ways humanity could spend its money, but I can't help myself. It's not so much the technology of moon-shots that excites me. It's the drama, the romance, the imagination, the sheer ambition of reaching for the stars. And staring up at the sky on a cloudless night blows my mind.

I know, of course, that each one of those twinkling points of light is actually a massive sun, sending its rays billions and billions of miles to reach my eyes, a journey that may have taken centuries. But looking up, I can't quite get my head around the fact that any two stars, which appear to me as neighbours just a smidgeon apart in the night sky, might actually be just as astonishingly far from each other as they are from me. Suddenly, I get a tiny sense of the scale of the cosmos, not as a fixed dome arching above me and my little world down here, but as an exploding three-dimensional space of almost infinite size, and one that's continuing to expand at vast speed even as I look at it. And that's just too much for me to take in.

The other question that fascinates me – like many rock fans whose formative years were spent listening to David Bowie in the 1970s, I suppose – is the one about *Life on Mars?* Viewing the astounding pictures sent back to Earth recently by the Mars Rover and its *Ingenuity* helicopter, I'm determined to live long enough to witness the day NASA brings back rock samples from the Red Planet for testing here on Earth, tests that may determine if indeed there was once life there. I've a decade or two to wait yet, so wish me luck!

Reading around the subject, though, I discovered an amazing fact the other day. There's a place on Mars named after a town in the Rhondda. I'll type that out for a second time, just in case you didn't take it in, or you can't quite believe your eyes...

There's a place on Mars named after a town in the Rhondda.

The place I'm talking about is one of 277 Martian craters which were named in the 1970s, just after Bowie killed off Ziggy Stardust, by the International Astronomical Union. The IAU's mission is to promote astronomical research, education and development through global cooperation. It bears official responsibility, on behalf of everyone on Earth, for naming features on other planets. And in August 1976, meeting in Grenoble, the IAU's Working Group for Planetary System Nomenclature decided that a crater in the Tritonis Lacus Region of Mars would be called... Porth.

That's right: Porth. And yes, it really is named after our Porth, the gateway to the Rhondda Valleys, the town where I went to secondary school. You can see it listed there, if you look up the Transactions of the International Astronomical Union for 1976. It takes its place in the alphabetical list of newly designated Tritonis Lacus craters, between the ones named for the towns of Phon in Thailand and Troika in Russia: 'Porth, UK (Wales)', says the official minute. If you're thinking of visiting, it's probably on Google Maps nowadays, but to save you the trouble, it's located at 21.4°N, 255.9°W. And, before you ask, Porth the Crater is 9.3 kilometres across. That's about the distance from our Porth to Maerdy.

Back in 1976, four other towns in the United Kingdom got a crater on Mars named after them, but Porth was the only one in Wales. One of the distinguished astronomers from all over the world who served on the Working Group for Planetary *etc.* was Tobias C Owen. He went on to become an author of both popular and highly specialised books about the planets and their atmospheres, and he played a significant role with NASA in guiding its early missions to Mars. Toby *Owen* – he must have had Welsh ancestry, surely... and that makes me wonder if he played a crucial part in labelling 'our' crater.

It's an interesting choice of a name, isn't it? 'Porth'. In Welsh, it's Y Porth, the gate or gateway – *porth* is a portal or a door, or in computer terminology, a device used to connect two different networks, a connection to the internet. And, yes, sitting there where the Rhondda Fawr meets the Rhondda Fach, Porth is our gateway, the portal to the Rhondda. It's a place of transition, a place you have to go through to get to somewhere else. I think of the thousands and thousands – the millions – of journeys Rhondda people have made through Porth over the years, some much more significant than others.

In the coal rush of Victorian times, the gateway to the Rhondda welcomed tens of thousands of new residents, all eager to share in the wealth the mines were creating.

In the Depression of the 1930s, tens of thousands were passing through Porth in the opposite direction, leaving 'Heartbreak Valley' forever to seek work in Slough or Reading, or some other distant English town, "having to sing their songs in a strange land", to quote the former Mayor of the Rhondda, Annie Powell. Yes, places so strange, so alien to the Rhondda, to its landscape and its values, that they might as well have been going to Mars.

And the comings-and-goings go on, to this very day: every working morning, every working evening, commuters negotiate the pinch-point of Porth; and families leave and newcomers arrive for the longer term.

Porth, of course, is more than just somewhere people pass through. It's home to 6,000 people and has a rich history of its own. One of its most fascinating stories – I've already told you about it – is that of William Evans, of Thomas and Evans grocers, and the genesis of the most successful brand ever to come out of the Rhondda: Corona pop.

But Porth was a gateway in another sense for me – the sense that the dictionary defines as 'a way of achieving something'. Hard work, they say, is the gateway to success. Porth was where I went to school, and I *did* work hard there – *honest*. But Porth County was more than a gateway to academic achievement. Lifelong friendships were formed with my classmates (even if some of them were on another planet!). And the school and its teachers opened doors for me to many things – storytelling and history and the Welsh language – which have remained close to my heart ever since.

In 1976, just as the Porth crater was being named, NASA's *Viking 1* lander was transmitting the first fuzzy images back to Earth from the Martian surface. It's tempting to wonder, now that the Red Planet is being mapped in high-definition digital detail, whether distinct areas of the crater will get names of their own: Birchgrove and Britannia, perhaps; Glynfach, Llwyncelyn, Mount Pleasant. And just beyond its edge, future Martian explorers might find their rovers trundling through Ynyshir or Trehafod, Cymmer, Dinas or Trealaw.

Is there life on Mars? There certainly is in Porth – a new transport hub, and now that Valleys Kids have taken over William Evans's old pop factory, a vibrant centre for youth arts and creativity of all kinds. As with my aspirations for Penygraig as a retail centre, as with what's already been achieved in Treorchy, let's hope we'll soon see a revival of Hannah Street, Porth – a revival of the glory days of Thomas and Evans fame, making the town once again a place with a name that's worth shouting to the ends of the earth… and way beyond the confines of our small planet.

Yes, why not? The lift-off of a stellar ambition: Porth – the Gateway to the Stars.

21

The Choir

I'M BOUND TO get into trouble with this chapter. Real hot water. But here goes...

You can't beat a good Welsh male voice choir. And amongst good Welsh male voice choirs – and here's where I'm heading for controversy – it's hard to beat Treorchy.

Now, I can already hear the howls of protest from the Rhondda Fach, from fans of Pendyrus, and fair enough. No one's going to deny that there's more than one Rhondda choir in the Super League of Welsh Male Ensembles. But I haven't said anything that's factually incorrect. It *is* hard to beat Treorchy. Back in the days when 20,000 people used to turn out to see who'd carry off the top choir prize at the National Eisteddfod, Treorchy won eight times in fifteen years. They've got class and they've got chutzpah, and I'll put it this way, as carefully as I can: amongst my favourite Rhondda choirs, there's none ahead of Treorchy.

I love choral singing, I do. But, like coalmines and rugby, there have been times when male voice choirs have been in danger of becoming a Welsh cliché. As the always-insightful Rhondda journalist and broadcaster Carolyn Hitt puts it, "For the past 40 years no English television producer has been capable of making a programme mentioning Wales without sticking a pile of old chaps on top of a mountain to croon 'We'll Keep a Welcome'."

Well, do you know what? As a TV producer, I've been close to being guilty of something very like that myself at times

– with both Treorchy and Pendyrus. And I was on location the day that my closest associate in programme-making, the inimitable Phil George, filmed the Treorchy Choir emerging one by one from the terraced doorsteps of Dumfries Street (the very street where Phil grew up) to join in glorious harmony, singing 'Myfanwy' in the middle of the road, to the amazement of all the neighbours. This early manifestation of what's become known as the 'flash-mob' may be a musical cliché, but it's one that's been seen and enjoyed by millions. I just checked – quite apart from its BBC broadcast, just one of the many pirated versions of the sequence posted on YouTube has been viewed 449,754 times and counting. The actor Joanna Lumley has said, "The Treorchy Male Choir's version of 'Myfanwy' is one of the most glorious things I've ever heard in all my long life." That's the thing about clichés: they can be popular – and good!

What makes Treorchy – and other Rhondda choirs – *more* than a cliché is their ability to reinvent themselves while staying true to their musical heritage. In Treorchy's case that heritage was forged by two remarkable men: the choir's first two conductors, who saw it through nearly half a century of growth and acclaim after it was re-formed in 1946. Both were schoolmasters, but they had very different personalities and styles. The first, John Haydn Davies, instilled an uncompromising musical discipline which transformed a band of raw and untrained recruits into an Eisteddfod-winning institution. In 1969, he handed the baton to John Cynan Jones, who took Treorchy onto the world stage, touring North America and Australia, singing in the finest concert halls and cathedrals in Britain, recording with EMI and appearing on radio and TV with superstars like Tom Jones, Julie Andrews, Ella Fitzgerald and Burt Bacharach.

Now, I wouldn't claim to know enough about the technicalities of the choral sound to be sure, but a friend of mine who *is* musical once explained Treorchy's magic to me like this: it was created by the *combination* of those first two conductors. John Haydn gave them the musical foundation, the drilling in tonic *sol-fa* that produced the precision of their sound. John Cynan built on that, and added an element of showmanship, of show business. Treorchy pioneered the introduction of the popular hits of the day into the male choir repertoire. By now, they've made nearly 60 commercial discs, and they're probably the most recorded male choir in the world. I don't mean to imply, of course, that John Cynan's musical credentials were anything but impeccable. He was a distinguished church organist in his own right; and at Treorchy Comprehensive, alongside the choir's long-serving accompanist, Jennifer Jones, he inspired the classical music education of a new generation of Upper Rhondda talent, like the choir's present conductor, Stewart Roberts. But any choir which has been invited to sing with Shirley Bassey, Ozzy Osbourne and Bon Jovi has been taught how to hit the right notes for the broad popular audience, as well as the musical cognoscenti.

Having given you some of the back story of the Treorchy choir, I want to finish by trying to put their sound in a context – a social context. And that allows me to redress the balance a bit. Because there's no doubt that the foremost chronicler of Welsh choral history is a man who sings with Pendyrus.

Professor Gareth Williams is a distinguished cultural historian, one of the leading interpreters of the industrial and social development of modern Wales. His book *Do You Hear The People Sing?* is a treasure trove which traces the origins and growth of choral singing in Wales from the nineteenth century to the present day. In it, Professor Williams brilliantly shows how communities dominated by heavy industry, and given a spiritual and musical lifeline by the chapel, provided the perfect springboard for a choral revolution. Wales's reputation as 'The Land of Song' may have begun with the triumph of the 'Côr Mawr', the Great South Wales Choir of men and women conducted by Caradog which carried off the One Thousand Guineas Challenge Cup in London's Crystal Palace in both 1872 and 1873. But it was the scores of male choirs – often linked to the workplace: the colliery, the quarry, the railway, the works, the docks – which established the tradition as a permanent, colourful and dramatic feature of national life. The crowds following the choirs were even greater in numbers than those supporting football teams. Eisteddfod competitions became 'choral bullfights', keenly honed rivalries spilling over into betting, missile throwing and assaults on adjudicators.

For the choristers themselves, performing could be a safety-valve, a much-needed psychological outlet. Men who did impossibly hard physical jobs, men who might struggle to express their emotions within the family circle or to close friends, felt no embarrassment in standing in front of thousands and singing from the heart about love, faith, joy and pain.

"And the emphasis," stresses Professor Williams, "as it was in industrial life itself, was on struggle, conflict, and the unity that hopefully would overcome all odds." Yes, it *was* the people's music. And in many ways, it still is.

In his book, Gareth Williams tells the story of Treorchy as magnanimously as he does that of his own choir, Pendyrus. His conclusion? We should cherish our Male Choirs – all of them – even more enthusiastically than we do. "They are the frequent object," he reminds us, "if not of scorn then of cliché, cartooned and caricatured near to death. Except they are far from dead, though their passing has been predicted for the last 60 years…The Welsh male voice choir is alive and well and impervious to cliché."

22

Llyn Fawr

I'M GOING TO start this chapter with one of the most unsurprising, commonplace statements you can possibly think of. Boring, you might well call it. But stay with me. Because it's led me back to something truly extraordinary – one of the greatest finds ever made within reach of the Rhondda.

A friend of mine posted a photo of herself on Facebook the other day.

"So what?" you're saying. Fair enough. I can't even claim it was a particularly good shot. To be honest, you needed some help just to spot her in the picture. "That's me in the red jacket," she felt obliged to point out.

She was proud of the photograph all the same. It showed her, you see, conquering one of her phobias. She was speeding, at 70 miles an hour, hundreds of feet above the Llyn Fawr reservoir on the Rhigos, thanks to Zip World Tower. The attraction is the fastest seated zip line in the world, according to the owners.

My friend did enjoy the experience, despite her anxieties, or so she claimed. Rather her than me, though. I'm not an adrenalin junkie, not a thrill-seeker – well, not of that kind anyway. Though that place – Llyn Fawr on the Rhigos – has given up a secret that really does take my breath away. And that's what I'm coming to.

Now, you know the place I'm talking about, don't you? Head up past Treorchy and into Treherbert. Then, instead of bearing left for Tynewydd, carry straight on, up the Rhigos mountain road – providing, of course, it hasn't been shut by snow, ice, rockfall or overly zealous council workmen. Keep going, and eventually you'll come to a viewing point with a fine panorama of the Bannau Brycheiniog (Brecon Beacons). Down below you is the old Tower Colliery, now the Zip World adventure hub. And to your left, nestled against Craig y Llyn, is a reservoir. Llyn Fawr: it just means 'Big Lake', and it's called that, I suppose, because there's a Llyn Fach, a 'Little Lake', just around the corner. My dad used to take me fishing at Llyn Fawr when I was a boy. The Upper Rhondda Angling Association still stocks it with what they call 'hard fighting rainbow and blue trout'. It was a natural lake before it was adapted for water supply. A few wild brown trout still swim there, or so I'm told.

The reservoir was created in 1909. At the time, the Rhondda was booming. Tens of thousands of people had moved in over the preceding 30 years, to work in the coalmines. This was 'American Wales', a modern industrial powerhouse, growing – as I've said – at a rate rivalled only by New York and Chicago. The River Rhondda, it was becoming obvious, didn't hold enough water for the burgeoning population's needs – even if it hadn't been turned black by coaldust. So the plan was to turn this natural lake the other side of the Rhigos into a reservoir, and then pump the water under Craig y Llyn, through a tunnel a mile and a quarter long under the mountain, to treatment works at Tynewydd. And that's what happened. The tunnel is still an important part of Welsh Water's infrastructure supplying the Rhondda, though it's well over a century old by now. There's a wonderful black-and-white photo which I'm guessing was taken not long before the work began – two men in suits and bowler hats with a horse and cart at the lake shore. I imagine them surveying, mapping out the necessary excavations.

Eventually, in deepening the lake to form the reservoir, workmen – in Dai caps rather than bowlers, I suppose –

cleared vegetation that had lain undisturbed for more than two and a half thousand years. And in doing that they made a fantastic discovery, one that still astounds me every time I think about it. What they found was buried in waterlogged peat, and so preserved in more or less mint condition since the late Bronze Age: a priceless hoard of weapons and tools. 21 metal objects altogether, all now kept safe in the National Museum in Cardiff. There are carpenters' tools: chisels and gouges. Axe heads. Horse harnesses and bits – some of the finest decorative horse tack ever found in Britain. And two spectacular cauldrons made from hammered sheets of bronze painstakingly pinned together with bossed bronze rivets. The cauldrons are so big that you can't get your arms around them.

But something else was found too, something else that thrills me. After all, I come from a family of 'notable Mid-Rhondda craftsmen', or so the *Rhondda Leader* said, in the obituary of my Grampa. He was the blacksmith at the Naval Colliery in Penygraig at the very time the Llyn Fawr discoveries came to light. I wonder what he'd have made of the iron sword, probably made in eastern France, which was found amongst the ancient hoard of treasure. From just one look at it, he'd have seen that the blade is superbly grooved – the quality of the craftsmanship telling him that this isn't a blacksmith's first-time effort with iron. This is a master at work, even though 2,700–2,800 years ago, iron was something really new. New and valuable – too valuable to have been left there in the lake without thought. From similar finds in bogs and rivers and lakes elsewhere, experts believe they're offerings to a local god or goddess. The reflective waters of the lake were regarded as a boundary between two worlds – our world, and Annwn, the Celtic underworld, where the gods held sway. These precious artefacts were given up to the deities below, payments in return for the hope of good harvests, mild winters or fortune in battle.

But how did these gifts to the waters come to be here in Wales in the first place? Are they evidence of trade or war?

50 or 60 years ago, an archaeologist looking at the Llyn Fawr collection would probably have said that the foreign sword was carried here by a hostile invader. Today, most experts tend to think that it was trade that brought it, the exchange of valued goods, passing perhaps through many hands, from the far continent to the hills of north Glamorgan.

Most intriguing of all to me, and I'm thinking of my grandfather again now, are two final objects amongst the discoveries: an L-shaped sickle and a short spearhead. When the museum analysed the ore in them, they found that they were made not in France or anywhere on the continent, but here, near where they were found. This is evidence that *local* smiths were beginning to transfer their skills in bronze to work in this even more useful new metal, iron. We have to imagine a bronze-smith somehow being introduced to or experimenting with the iron ores that you can find in the geology of the rocks of the Rhigos: experimenting with smelting, forging the iron and creating new metal objects in the old, familiar style of bronze work. So these finds herald a whole new era in the human history of these islands: we're in the dawn of native ironworking, not just in Wales but in the whole of Britain and Ireland, because these are the oldest native-made iron objects ever found here. So the 'Llyn Fawr Phase' has become the official name of the beginning of the Iron Age in Britain, between 800 and 600 years Before Christ.

And it's called that all because Tommy John, my Grampa – and tens of thousands of other Rhondda people who may be *your* ancestors – needed clean drinking water.

23

Streets Ahead

Yawn! I'm late getting up today. A Saturday morning lie-in. But then, I *am* a growing teenager.

Imagine, two generations back there was no such thing as a teenager. Children just got on with it, and grew up. I'd have been working down the pit by now. But this is the 1970s! Everyone stays in school until they're at least 15, and some of us go on beyond that again.

Anyway, the 1970s won't last forever. I better get a move on. I need to go up to Tonypandy Library and take my book back, and it closes at noon. So come on, let's go. Down the road, past the Adare and the Plaza to the lights.

Look, there's Steve, Auntie Dot's boy, going into Oxford House. I wonder if he's after sweets – or *cigarettes*? He's at that awkward in-between age. I like Oxford House, but we don't get our *Western Mail* and *Rhondda Leader* from there. We have them delivered from Ivens's in Penygraig, our papers.

The lights have changed. We can cross Trinity Hill. There's Cosy Corner and, next door, Hathaway's. Someone was telling me the other day that the little lift they've got behind the counter that takes the plates of fish and chips up to the first floor is called a dumb waiter. Funny name.

Plenty more shops in this block. Wallpaper. Washing machines. 'Pandy's busy this morning. Always is on a Saturday. There's Robert Rees's mother from up the street. And my friend Gareth Richards from Hendrecafn, popping into The Calypso for a game on the flipper. Funny smells in that café sometimes. What exactly is wacky baccy anyway? I've got an order to drop into Shirley's cake shop for Mam. I'll pick it up on the way back. I'll ask Auntie Marian, who serves there, to add a custard slice to the list, just for me.

Past Ebenezer and the police station. Jones the Saddler's. Smells of satchels in there, wallets, all kinds of leather stuff. Rugby boots too, and sports kit. Mr Jones is a proper Welsh speaker. His daughter goes to Rhydfelen. Very pretty, freckles and red hair. Nerys, her name is, I think. But she's a couple of years older than me, so I can forget that.

Woolworths coming up. Is that my friend Julie going in there? Wonder what for. Just saying hello, probably, to our other friend Julie, who's got a Saturday job on the tills…

Across the road, by the Empire Café, there's Keith Swayne, my Uncle Len's butty. He's going into Don Taylor's – he'll get served by my friends Alan and Andrew Coombes from Hughes Street. Saturday jobs they've got too, ringing up the groceries.

On this side, Hodge's, the men's outfitters. Very old fashioned. Uncle Len shops in there. Here's another café, the Central. Full this morning. Still a bit early for fish and chips, I'd say. "Alright butt?… Not bad, mun." No idea who that was. But you just say hello to everyone, don't you? Acknowledging people as you pass by is natural in the Rhondda, not like down Cardiff.

We're coming up to Bethel, now. Here's Boots, next to the White Hart. *O, dammo*, I've got a roll of film I meant to send away to get developed. I'll have to pop back in the week. I need a new bottle of that Brut aftershave too.

Let's cross again. Barclays Bank. The Wishing Well – cards and gifts and books. Nice selection of paperbacks, if you've got the money to buy. The library is free, mind, so let's wait. *Morning, Mrs Davies!* Gladys Davies, that was: goes to chapel with my parents. Just got her Sunday joint from the butcher's, by the looks of it. Her husband, David Davies, 'Dai Twice', works for the Gas Board. She'll be cooking on gas tomorrow.

Another department store. Clothes and knick-knacks. Fancy goods. Toys as well. My Grampa used to work in there. Leslie Stores. He'd been pensioned off as the colliery blacksmith at 65, but he told a lie about how old he was and got a job there as a storeman. Eventually, on the day they thought he'd reached retirement age, they threw him a special farewell party. He was *seventy*-five by then.

On again. Barney Isaacs, the jewellers, across the road. Hilda's, the florist's. Now we're coming up to Knill and Thomas, the pet shop. One of my friends – better not say who – went in there with a gang of us one Saturday, hiding a slice of raw carrot up his sleeve. He'd cut the carrot into the shape of a goldfish. Quick as a flash, he dips his hand into the fish tank, and pulls it out again, making a big show of holding up this orange shape, and stuffing it straight into his gob and eating it front of the horrified serving staff! He scarpered out of the shop door before they could catch him. We're not going in there today.

Let's have a look in the window of Spice instead. Now, here are some clothes worth considering. Proper 1970s fashion, as trendy as anything you could buy in Carnaby Street. Ben Sherman shirts, checked with button-down collars. Levi's and Wranglers. Pinstripe suits with big wide lapels and flared trousers even wider. Maybe I'll be able to afford them one day.

On again. Past the barbers and a couple more shops we go – Farmer's, women's clothes and sewing things. Here's the library at last. We can get a frothy coffee up in Melardi's afterwards, say hello to Lui and Tereza and June, then walk on past Times Furnishing to Mal Rees's record shop. Bob Scourfield will be in there, I bet, and Andrew Shurey (*surely!*). And my best butty John Thomas from Ystrad – he'll have got there early, even before they opened, probably. He can't wait to see if Mal has got that new Emerson, Lake and Palmer album in. Wonder if he'll be a 'Lucky Man' today, ha, ha.

But, c'mon, the library shuts at 12, and I've got to return this book. *The Lord of the Rings*. Long read, it was. A bit backward-looking as a story, but they should make a film of it, I reckon. Still, I fancy something more futuristic to read now – science fiction. Isaac Asimov, he's the boy. He writes about the robots we'll all have pretty soon to do all the work for us, and massive computers that run everything, so we can just lounge around and enjoy ourselves. I'm looking forward to 1980! And if they haven't got any Asimov, my cousin Ceri will recommend something. She's the librarian.

Well, that's it, our walk up through Tonypandy's done. I'm all worn out and I didn't even go into any of those shops. It was more a social experience than a retail one, if you know what I mean.

It's strange, but going on about sci-fi has made me wonder about Dunraven Street – what it'll be like in the distant future, 50 years from now, say. If I could time-travel, I could go and have a dekko, I suppose. All those shops will be selling stuff from the twenty-first century. But they'll still be here, of course.

Won't they?

24

Uncle Len: The Rhondda Working Man

DID YOU HAVE a family member who was *different* to all the rest of you? Lots of Rhondda families did. We did. I've just mentioned him in that last chapter: Uncle Len. There'd be those in Penygraig who remember him still. He had a wicked sense of humour and a fondness for company (sometimes on licensed premises). And he was always causing trouble, or at least stirring things up a bit. In a tidy, respectable, chapel-going family like ours, one that erred on the side of being a little too puritan and straightlaced, Uncle Len stood out as an original, a one-off. But in the wider community, there were thousands of Rhondda men who spent their lifetimes toiling in unimaginably tough jobs, but retained their charactistic intelligence, their quirky individuality. So the chances are, even if you didn't know Len, you knew someone cut from the same cloth. He was the epitome of the Rhondda Working Man. But he was also, unmistakeably, himself: Uncle Len.

I loved my Uncle Len. But there's no two ways about it: he could be one of the most contrary, cantankerous, cussed customers you would ever meet. He loved arguing. Rugby, politics, religion, the weight of the moon – the subject didn't matter. He just loved starting arguments. And he *really* loved it when they went on... and on. To make sure they did, just when the steam was going out of the dispute, he'd change his opinion, whatever it was, and adopt the polar opposite position to the one he'd started with, which confused and frustrated everyone else involved, and started the whole thing up again.

"I don't want no fuss," he would often say. But a fuss is usually what he caused, and I suspect what he really craved.

It's hard for me to imagine my Uncle Len when he was young. I mean, people were always saying about him, "*Duw*, he's a boy, aye!" But he really was a boy once. There's a famous story of him, as a nipper, getting on the wrong side of the policeman who lived a few doors away from the family home on Tylacelyn Road. He gave Len a telling off for something *Len* swore he didn't do. As if. So Len upped the ante by marching down the back lane and defacing the copper's back gate, by daubing black pitch all over it. Typical of Len. Did he think no-one would notice? And, of course, typical of Len to do it so obviously that he got found out.

Len left school – Craig-yr-Eos Secondary Modern – at 14. He joined his father, my grandfather, Tommy John, in the Naval Colliery to be taught his trade as a blacksmith. Later, they both had a spell at Brown Lenox in Pontypridd, making anchor chains for the big ocean liners. By the time I was born, Len was a welder in the steelworks in Port Talbot. He was a strong man, as you'd expect from the places he worked in and the jobs he did, but he'd always 'suffered with his nerves', as they said back then. In his fifties, he had what I suppose was a sort of breakdown. He came back to the Rhondda and my parents took him in, which wasn't unusual in the Valleys at the time. Once he was back on his feet, still living with us, he took up a whole new career. It wasn't a soft option. He got a job in Trealaw – as a gravedigger.

Sharing a house with Len would try the patience of a saint, even one as long-suffering as my mother. His nerviness manifested itself in flippant or contradictory answers to any question put to him, any small courtesy or offer of help. Time and again, he baulked at Mam's gentle kindness towards him.

One morning, over breakfast, he went too far in winding her up, and she snapped. In a totally uncharacteristic flash of frustration, mild-mannered Mam threw her full bowl of cornflakes at him. It went all over his cardigan – and down in family legend.

Len was often hyper at breakfast-time. Once, we were all on holiday together in foreign parts: Bournemouth. The prim-and-proper guest house had never seen anyone like him. And in no time, Len had decided its middle-class reticence needed a good shaking up. On the second morning, he stomped into the crowded, whispering breakfast room, announcing – declaiming – "Dreadful news!" He waited, theatrically, until all heads were turned in his direction. "*Tom Jones is dead!*" Coffee cups rattled. Butter knives clattered onto tabletops. Stunned Home Counties matrons fought back tears. *Oh, yes,* says Len, gravely, *he slipped and fell on the Green, Green Grass of Home.*

Back when Len lived in Port Talbot, freed from the steelworks by a happy pattern of shift work, he'd spend his summer days following the cricket at St Helens. There he saw the legendary Gary Sobers strike his six sixes in one over. When Sobers came back the following season, Uncle Len took me to watch him play. At tea, Len headed off towards the changing rooms carrying the half-size cricket bat he'd given me the previous Christmas, already inscribed with the signatures of the entire Glamorgan team, Len's heroes. Five minutes later, Len returned. The greatest all-rounder's autograph had been added to the back of the bat: Garfield Sobers. How had Uncle Len managed it?

"Oh, I know the man who minds the changing-room door," he said, nonchalantly. Len knew everyone.

But what did Sobers say?

"He said, 'Oh, man, can't I ever get no peace?'"

"*So what happened then?*" I asked my uncle, rather shocked.

Len shrugged and replied, "I just said, '*Give me peace*: that's what I say too. And that's what this little boy with no mammy or daddy is always telling me.'"

That was me – instantly, falsely orphaned to blackmail a cricketing titan into giving an autograph. But Sobers was one of *my* heroes. And I was the only boy in the whole of Glamorgan with the great man's signature on the back of his bat. I decided not to feel guilty.

Speaking of heroes, to me – and Len would think I'd gone soft in the head if he could hear me saying this – there was something heroic about Uncle Len himself. *The labourer is worthy of his hire*, the Bible says; Len's decades of hard toil gave him not just a powerful body, but also a stature and a dignity, a *worth*, in my eyes.

He was still living at home with us when I got my first job. I was 21, fresh out of college. I arrived home after that first day in the office, practically collapsing onto the sofa, making a big show of holding my hand out pathetically for Mam to put a reviving mug of tea into it. *I'd had a tough day! I was a proper man now too, doing proper work!*

Len was lounging in the armchair opposite, home from his shift in the cemetery, cruising through the *Western Mail* crossword. He'd left Craig-yr-Eos without any qualifications, but he could finish that fiendishly difficult cryptic puzzle faster than anyone I knew, and twice as quick as me, a grammar school swot and a supposed English scholar. Anyway, he clocked what was going on, all the *fuss* I was making about having done a whole day's work… in an office! He lowered the paper.

"Don't worry, boy…" he counselled me sagely. "The first 40 years are the worst."

Len did his 40 years, and more. I think of him, his working man's physique, his fine broad chest. I remember the words he spoke and the places he loved and the things he did. And I bring to mind that whole generation of working-class Rhondda men, how they toiled and laboured. To me, they *are* heroes. Their sweat fashioned our world, fashioned the world from which all our more famous heroes sprang. They were strong, but so many of them – so many – had their health broken by the work they did. Few of them enjoyed a long and hale retirement. And the rewards they got in the things of this world were pitiful.

Uncle Len passed away as a Millennium ended. He went suddenly: at a quarter past midnight on 1 January, 2000. Typical of him. There was the Queen and Tony Blair and the Dome and the millions spent on celebrations and fireworks. Who but Len could manage to upstage it all in our minds and our memories?

I spoke at Uncle Len's funeral, quoting something I've mentioned earlier in this book – but it's worth repeating now. Those words of another of Len's heroes, Richard Burton, speaking of the death of *his* friend and fellow actor, Ferndale's Stanley Baker: that there was a class of Welshman, 'almost all from the Rhondda Valley', who were 'original and unique to themselves, powerful and loud and dangerous and clever.' There weren't enough of them, mourned Burton, and it wasn't fair that another had been taken away.

That was Len, and that was how I felt about him, to a T. To him, and to all those other powerful, loud, dangerous, clever Rhondda heroes like him, ordinary men who did back-breaking work, the men of your family and mine, original and unique – we all owe a huge, huge debt. Let's remember them with pride.

25

Druids Close to Home

CAN YOU PICTURE Druids Close in Treorchy?

It's a little crescent of houses over on the Cwmparc side of the valley, off the New Road, near the turning for the Bwlch. One of my very best schoolfriends lives there these days. In fact, she was my girlfriend for a short while...

But it's not her I meant to talk about. It's the Stones.

Not The Rolling Stones. Though there were times I used to dance to their music with her... *O, daro*, I've got all confused and sentimental now. I'll start again...

Can you picture Druids Close in Treorchy? If you're familiar with the area, you'll know that the modern houses are built around a circle of a dozen standing stones. They look like some sort of ancient Celtic monument. It's not a mini-Stonehenge, though: they're *Gorsedd* Stones, put up there to mark the fact that the National Eisteddfod was held in Treorchy in 1928. They're where the Archdruid presided over the druidic ceremonies of the festival, hence the name of the Close. You can find a Gorsedd Circle like it in most Welsh towns or cities that have hosted the Eisteddfod, though this one is unique in the Rhondda, because it's the only time the 'National' has come here. Yes, I know that Pontypridd will host it in 2024, to the delight of its many supporters locally, but us Rhondda folk are pretty particular about 'Ponty': we love the town, but though it may be part of Rhondda Cynon Taf, strictly speaking it *isn't* in the Rhondda. All the same, although the Eisteddfod has visited the Rhondda 'proper' just the once, the valley's got plenty of connections with this centrepiece of Welsh-language culture. Some of them will surprise you.

The National Eisteddfod is a kind of Olympics for Welsh-speakers, the pinnacle of the cultural calendar. It's held every year – when there's not a pandemic on – at the beginning of August. Each year, the huge Pavilion and myriad surrounding marquees travel to a different part of Wales, giving a real boost to the language in the area, with a ten-day spectacular of music and arts, dance and song and ceremony. Tens of thousands come to see who's won the big Eisteddfod competitions, especially the Crown and the Chair awarded to the best poets – or they come simply to have a good chinwag in Welsh with friends and acquaintances they bump into every year around the Eisteddfod field, a tradition known as *crwydro'r Maes*.

Tradition is important in the Eisteddfod – the whole Gorsedd thing is a tradition in itself. Like most traditions, it was invented, mainly by a strange man from the Vale of Glamorgan called Edward Williams. Better known by his bardic name, Iolo Morganwg, he loved ancient Welsh manuscripts. He loved them so much that if they didn't exist, he forged them himself. Claiming he was reviving an age-old rite, Iolo held a Gorsedd or Gathering of Bards at the Rocking Stone on Pontypridd Common back in 1814. Some say that it was Iolo himself who constructed the circle of stones around the big central one. After all, he was a stonemason by trade.

By the beginning of the twentieth century, Iolo's bardic gathering had morphed into something much more like the Eisteddfod we know today. Something of its importance can be judged by the fact that when the 1928 National Eisteddfod came to Treorchy, *two* British Prime Ministers attended.

No surprise, I suppose, that David Lloyd George – a proud Welsh-speaker – was there. There's a famous photo of DLG at the Treorchy Eisteddfod, with his wife Margaret and daughter Megan, and little Evie Williams from Ferndale who won the folk song competition. Lloyd George had left Downing Street by then, but the man who was in residence at No. 10 in 1928 was also on the *Maes*. I wonder what Prime Minister Stanley Baldwin, born into a prosperous English family and educated at Harrow and Cambridge, made of Treorchy and the Eisteddfod. Whatever he thought privately, he's reported to have praised the Rhondda people for organising the event at a time of huge poverty and economic depression here – which, some might point out, his policies did little to alleviate.

Every Eisteddfod takes on something of the character of the place that's hosting it, and Treorchy's was no exception. The Eisteddfod Chair was presented by a coalmining community, though a far-from-local one. It came from the Blackstone Welsh Society of Queensland in Australia. And in a striking innovation that year, the Arts and Crafts section of the Eisteddfod added Science to its remit. It was done specifically because the festival was in Treorchy, with an emphasis on mining and Rhondda geology and geography, as well as crafts associated with the coal industry. Science and Technology remain big features of the Eisteddfod to this day, with a so-called 'Village' on the Eisteddfod site dedicated to them. We can think of it as Rhondda's gift to the National Eisteddfod.

Almost half a century after that Treorchy Eisteddfod, Nonconformist ministers from the Rhondda scooped the Eisteddfod Crown three times in seven years. Haydn Lewis, the pastor of Jerusalem, Ton Pentre won twice – in Rhosllannerchrugog in 1961 and again in Barry in 1968. His son, Richard Lewis, became a distinguished television drama producer. 'Dic' Lewis, as I knew him as a senior colleague when I joined the BBC, always made a point of mentioning proudly his Rhondda roots and his education at Porth County.

123

But my favourite Eisteddfod poem, as I've mentioned before, has to be *Y Ffynhonnau*, which won the Crown for another Rhondda minister, Rhydwen Williams, in the 1964 National. *Y Ffynhonnau* ('The Mountain Springs' in English – remember?) recounts the whole history of the valley, from its rural past to the coming of the coalmines and then the decline of the industry. It's not at all what you'd expect from an Eisteddfod-winning poem: it's not bardic or druidic or highfalutin in any way, though it does have some lovely lyric passages, and it ends with an old miner delighting in the fact that his neighbour's daughter is being sent to Ysgol Gymraeg Ynyswen, the new Welsh-language junior school at the top of the valley. Mostly, it's written in the ordinary voices of the Rhondda, a soundscape of boxers and jazz-band musicians and choristers and Welsh-speaking budgies and parents who snap at their children (*cae'r blydi drws 'na!*): characters who are proud that the valley has left its mark on them, like a brand on livestock, in their accents and memories and beliefs. It's a quote I use in my own social media profile: *Mae marc y cwm fel nod ar ddafad arnaf. Acen. Atgofion. Cred.* So many of us might say the same: it's the Rhondda that's shaped us into who we are, through and through. No wonder I was inspired to use the text of the poem as the script of that hour-long TV film I made, celebrating the valley I cherish as deeply as Rhydwen Williams did.

Fast forward half a century again, and it was Rhondda *women* making an impact at the Eisteddfod, and not before time! Manon Rhys won the Crown in 2015. She's the daughter of James Kitchener Davies, 'Kitch', a legendary Rhondda educationalist and champion of the Welsh language. Manon was one of the first pupils in that school in Ynyswen, before going on to Porth County. She's written novels set in the Rhondda, as well as poetry. One of them, *Rara Avis*, is about – amongst other things – the oddity of being raised in her generation as a thoroughly Welsh-speaking Rhondda child.

Christine James from Tonypandy also went to Porth County, but her home background, much like mine, was English-speaking. She not only won the Crown at the 2005 National Eisteddfod, but she went on to become Archdruid of Wales in 2013 – so it was Christine who crowned her friend Manon Rhys at the 2015 Festival, a memorable moment for them both, and for the Rhondda's place in Eisteddfodic history. I remember Christine well as a schoolgirl – Christine Mumford she was then, and her parents were friends of my Mam and Dad. She was the first woman to become Archdruid and the first Archdruid ever *not* to have been a Welsh-speaker from early childhood: a living embodiment of the idea that the Eisteddfod – like the language itself – belongs to us all, not just to those who are brought up speaking Welsh.

And that's something worth remembering the next time you're passing Druids Close.

26

In the Magpie's Nest

I WAS BORN... *in a magpie's nest.* Yes, you read that right: *a magpie's nest.* It's a strange thing to say, I know. But it's the truth. Chances are, if you're roughly the same dap as me (as we say in the Valleys for people of a similar age) and you grew up in the Rhondda, *you* were born in a magpie's nest too.

I'm quite proud of the fact, to be honest. I mean, it's got more polish, a bit more *graen* to it than saying you were born in a workhouse. Though, now I come to think about it, it's sort of true that I was born in a workhouse...

Am I speaking in riddles again? Fair enough. Give me a moment and I'll explain.

I had to fill in a form this morning. One of those online things. And there it was, an empty box: *Place of birth...* I'm always scrupulously honest on these forms, and though I think of myself as a Penygraig boy, through and through, born and bred, I'm not really. My actual entry into this world, like almost all the other Rhondda children of my generation was in... Llwynypia. That's what it says on my birth certificate, so it must be true.

It's there on my passport too: *Place of birth/Lieu de naissance: Llwynypia.*

It's a great thing to have on a passport or any official document. Because if any officious official starts questioning you, and they come from anywhere beyond Offa's Dyke, they look at the word 'Llwynypia' and more or less give up before they've found what they think is the first vowel. Llwynypia.

Llwyn-y-pia. Llwyn is literally a bush in Welsh, but when a bird's name is mentioned next to it – in this case *pia*, a magpie – then you can take *llwyn* to mean 'nest'. *Llwyn-y-pia* – the magpie's nest. And, of course, the reason that I – like so many other Rhondda people – was born 'in the magpie's nest', is because Llwynypia Hospital was, for many years, the maternity hospital for the whole valley.

But where does the workhouse come into it?

The Rhondda's coalmines first opened up when Queen Victoria was on the throne. There was no such thing as the welfare state. If people couldn't work – because they were ill, injured, or simply old – and their family couldn't support them, they had to turn to the Parish for assistance. Often, they were sent to the dreaded workhouse. It was a harsh system, infamous for forced child labour, malnutrition, beatings and neglect. Put simply, the combination of punishing workload and poor diet killed many of the inmates. It was Charles Dickens who helped to open the eyes of the Victorian public to the evils of the workhouse, in his novel *Oliver Twist*. Dickens described how children were mistreated and underfed, with poor Oliver uttering the immortal request: *"Please, sir, I want some more."*

The first workhouse anywhere near the Rhondda opened on the Graig in Pontypridd in 1865. By the end of that century, with the inrush of people to the coalfield, it was far too small to cope with the need. So the Board of Guardians bought 25 acres of land at Llwynypia to build a new workhouse. It was opened in 1903. Accommodation, behaviour and diet there were subject to the usual strict discipline, but social norms in the new century were *somewhat* more enlightened than in Dickens's heyday, and the new institution was described as 'a home for the destitute, chronic sick and elderly'. Able-bodied inmates were put to work in the kitchen, the laundry or on the smallholding on the site, tending fruit and veg and cereals. Chickens, goats and pigs were kept there too, and they needed looking after as well. They may indeed have been treated better than the human residents.

It wasn't until 1927 that the workhouse became a proper hospital. The inmates were moved out, though one of them – a Mr Chris Jordan – was given a hospital bed, and he stayed on there at Llwynypia for decade after decade, until he died, as astonishingly recently as 1986.

Meanwhile, it took some time for Rhondda people to get used to the idea that what had been a Poor Law Infirmary was now treating general patients, not just the destitute. Gradually, the facilities at the site were modernised – with an operating theatre, a pathology lab and a radiology (X-ray) department. In 1930, Glamorgan County Council took over the hospital from the Board of Guardians, and this is when maternity facilities were properly introduced, so that the hospital could be recognised as a training school by the Central Midwives Board.

During the Second World War, part of the hospital was dedicated to the treatment of wounded servicemen, so maternity was moved out again, across the valley to Glyncornel House, which was acquired from the Powell Duffryn coal combine for the purpose.

After the war, on 5 July 1948, the National Health Service was born. Llwynypia Hospital got a new lease of life. Facilities were upgraded again. In the 1950s, physiotherapy and casualty departments opened, together with a new, modern maternity unit. And this is where I come in – just about!

My Mam was 30 when I was born – quite old for a first-time mother in those days. My parents weren't so fortunate as to own such a thing as a motorcar; so our neighbour next-door-but-one on Tylacelyn Road kindly agreed to take my mother the couple of miles up to the hospital in his car when the time came. Maldwyn Jones was a responsible businessman – he owned a printing company in Tonypandy – but he and his wife Elsie didn't have children of their own, and I think he must have been slightly panicked when my mother knocked at the door, already in labour.

Fathers didn't usually attend births back then. So it was just Mam-to-be and Maldwyn speeding through 'Pandy in the car; and me, baby John, ready to appear on the scene at any moment. But, when he got to Glyncornel Lake, panicked Maldwyn turned *left*. He was zooming up through the woods to Glyncornel House before my mother – who was understandably distracted by other matters – realised his mistake. Maldwyn was taking her to the old maternity unit. But that was now a geriatric ward.

Some children are born old, so they say, but I wasn't ready to join the elderly chronic sick on day one! Thankfully, Maldwyn managed to turn the car around and get Mam to Llwynypia, just in time for me to make my grand entrance. I've got a black-and-white photo taken on the maternity ward to prove it – three medical staff in starched aprons holding me and two other bonny Rhondda newborns up for the camera. I wonder where those other two babies are now – if you were born in Llwynypia on 10 July 1957, please get in touch and let me know.

Fast forward to my teenage years, and Llwynypia Hospital features for another reason: the first protest march I ever went on. It was impressive, mind – thousands demonstrating against the closure of the casualty unit at Llwynypia, the only facility like it in the Rhondda. The Health Board was planning to centralise emergency services far away at the East Glamorgan Hospital in Church Village, beyond Pontypridd. On a sunny afternoon, we paraded from the hospital gates on Partridge Square, down through 'Pandy and on to a public meeting in the famous Judge's Hall, where many rallies and political debates had been held over the years. Down through Dunraven Street we marched: nurses and miners, doctors and housewives, schoolchildren like myself, carrying banners, chanting... and singing, to the tune of 'Tipperary':

Up the Rhondda!

> It's a long way to East Glamorgan, it's a long way to go.
> It's a long way to East Glamorgan, and the roads are awful slow.
> Goodbye Llwynypia, farewell Partridge Square,
> It's a long, long way to East Glamorgan –
> You're dead 'fore you're there.

Those words from the early 1970s have stuck in my mind for half a century: such a pointed and clever adaptation. I've always wondered who thought them up, and how all of us marchers got to learn them. It was a glorious cause. But a total failure. The 'rationalisation' went ahead anyway. All that was left for in-patients at Llwynypia in its last years were the bookends of life – the geriatric wing, and that famous maternity unit. Even they went in the end. Now, of course, the buildings are gone too. There's a spanking new hospital, Ysbyty Cwm Rhondda, not far from Partridge Square. But for me, and I guess for thousands of other Rhondda people who began life there too, it will always be that old institution up on the hill that will be dear to the heart. I may have been born in a magpie's nest, one that used to be a workhouse, and nearly, nearly on a geriatric ward. But thanks to Llwynypia Hospital, I can say it proudly: I'm a Rhondda boy.

27
Railway Lines

IT'S QUIZ TIME with *John on the Rhondda*...

Let's play *Name the Odd One Out*. Here's a list of Rhondda places: Trehafod, Porth, Dinas, Tonypandy, Llwynypia, Ystrad, Ton Pentre, Treorchy, Treherbert. Now, *Name the Odd One Out!*

Well, if you know the valley at all well, you may have worked out that these are all Rhondda railway stations. But which one's *the Odd One Out*?

I'd say it was Ton Pentre, because when I was growing up, there wasn't a train station called 'Ton Pentre'. But then you could argue that *the Odd One Out* is Ystrad, because when I was growing up, there wasn't a station in Ystrad – it was *called* Ystrad but it was *in* Ton Pentre. Confused? Some visitors certainly must have been!

I wonder who it was who came up with the bright idea of calling the station in Ton Pentre 'Ystrad Station'. Whoever it was, I'm pretty sure they went on to a glittering career labelling routes for budget airlines. You know, when they tell you you're flying to Paris and you end up hundreds of kilometres away in a tiny airport somewhere in the French countryside; or when you've planned a short break in Stockholm only to discover you've landed in an obscure town in Denmark instead.

Well, no, I haven't actually done any of that either; but you know what I mean – until 1986, Ystrad Station just *wasn't* in Ystrad.

A trip by train was always a treat for me – but then I'm lucky enough never to have had to commute on the 07.27 from Treherbert. Yes, trains are delights for me. And nostalgic, too. They always remind me of Mam and Dad... and swimming. Let me tell you why.

Trains remind me of *Dad* because when I was very small and just learning to read, my father had to work away from home for a couple of months. Every week he'd post me one of the *Thomas the Tank Engine* books – the original ones, long before it was ever put on TV. Dad had begun his working life in Llanharry and every day he travelled back and forth – I don't think they called it 'commuting' then – from Penygraig station on the old Ely Valley line. There was only a tiny group of regular passengers and if Dad was ever late in the morning, the guard would hold the train until he got there. Personal service. But the service came to a full stop in 1958. There's a photo of the last train at the platform in Penygraig. I can't spot Dad in it, though I'm sure he must have been there. Coal trains went on using the track until the Cambrian Colliery closed. By then a gang of us boys used to walk the line all the way from Penygraig to go swimming in the smart new indoor pool in Tonyrefail. By now, of course, that track is a road, nose to tail every morning with commuters' cars heading for Cardiff. That's progress for you.

Trains remind me of *Mam* because sometimes she'd take me on one of her shopping trips to Cardiff. We'd catch the train from 'Pandy station. 'Tonypandy *and Trealaw*' it was called then. Though a bit like Ystrad Station, it wasn't close to the centre of either Tonypandy or Trealaw. Not that Trealaw has really got a centre. Or has it? (I'm fighting off the temptation to tell that old gag about the dead centre of Trealaw being the cemetery, but that's as corny as calling the club opposite the cemetery gates 'The Rez' – and sadly, just like my joke, the Resurrection Club has recently died a death. The building stands derelict.)

I've completely lost my train of thought now. Gone way off track. Right off the rails. Train... Track... Rails... *Ah, yes.* I was at Tonypandy and Trealaw station with my Mam. I can still see the chocolate-and-cream-coloured signs, the little booking office up at the level of Bridge Street, the steep, steep steps down to the platforms. Yes, *two* platforms in those days. And three tracks: Up and Down, and the middle line for coal trains. A siding for goods, too. Just like the proper railways I'd read about in those *Thomas the Tank* books.

So we're on our way to Cardiff. I'd be checking off the stations. They're still imprinted in my memory: *Dinas. Porth. Trehafod. Pontypridd. Treforest. Treforest Estate. Taffs Well. Radyr. Llandaff (for Whitchurch). Queen Street. Cardiff General.*

I didn't know then that the Taff Vale Railway, in addition to carrying millions of tons of best Rhondda steam coal to Cardiff Docks, was famous for a trades union dispute which led to the foundation of the Labour Party. No, my mind was on whether – after Mam had done all her shopping – we'd have time for lunch in The Louis, or for a swim in the Empire Pool opposite the station. I rarely missed out. Afterwards, loaded with bags, we'd get back on the train and Mam would *always* make sure to point out the waterfall at Radyr on the way home. Why was she so particular about that? It's a nice view, but all the same. Maybe it was because of that white water tumbling over the fall – she wanted me to see that a river didn't have to be black, like it was back home in the Rhondda.

When I was old enough to take the train by myself, there was another swimming connection. On sunny summer days I used to take the train to Pontypridd with my junior school friends – Paul Dodd, Gareth Richards, Dilwyn Jenkins maybe, or Alan and Andrew Coombes – to go swimming outdoors in Ynysangharad Park. This was years before they restored the Lido and it became so trendy that you have to book in advance to swim there, of course. 'Ponty Pool' we called it, which always confused me when my Grampa talked about a certain rugby team – *they* were from the *Gwent* valleys.

Anyway, we'd spend hours in the water, until we'd start shivering and the flesh on our fingers was all shrivelled and white, not to mention other bits of ourselves... and then back we'd run, to that huge station platform – was it really the longest one in Britain?

Sometimes, we'd get up to a bit of mischief on the way home. Not that we were bold enough to pull the communication cord. No! 'Penalty for Improper Use: £50', warned the sign, an unimaginable fortune *none* of our families could have afforded. But we would do something that was just a teensy bit naughty. We'd *deliberately jump on the wrong train*. The one that took the fork just outside Ponty station that led to Merthyr Tydfil. Merthyr! How exotic! We'd get a free ride all the way to the end of the line, protesting our innocence to the guard, before returning all the way to Pontypridd and taking the *right* train this time, the Treherbert train, back to Tonypandy and Trealaw.

Strangely, I can never remember travelling *up* the valley by train. It was always *buses* to Blaencwm or Blaenrhondda. When I was a young teenager, my best friend lived up in Ystrad, on Tyntyla Road near the Star Hotel. If there'd there been a station close by, it would have been handy. But back then Ystrad station was still in Ton Pentre.

These days, I love taking the train to Treorchy – the station's so convenient for all those lovely shops and cafés on the high street. But I've still never travelled by rail to Ynyswen, which was opened (like the 'new' Ystrad station) in 1986, nor all the way to Treherbert... and I never got to go beyond what's now the end of the line. I always regret missing the chance to go further – through the tunnel to Blaengwynfi, and down to the coast, on the Rhondda and Swansea Bay Railway. What a thrill that would have been for a boy brought up on *Thomas the Tank Engine* stories. Two miles, just about, in darkness, under the mountain! But they closed the tunnel when I was 10, and since then services have had to terminate at Treherbert. Still, thanks to the sterling efforts of the Rhondda Tunnel Society, and their campaign to reopen it as a cycle and pedestrian route, one day I might make that spine-tingling journey through to the Afan Valley, even if it's not on a train.

I'm not certain I'll be up to cycling all the way down to the beach at Aberavon, mind you. But if I do, I'll make sure to pack my bathers... in memory of Mam and Dad and all those swimming connections.

28

Rhondda Billionaires

YOU BETTER WATCH out! I'm giving you fair warning. *Gan bwyll, gwd boi!* I've got my dander up. Tamping, I am.

See, I was just listening to the radio, and I heard this bloke on the news describe some other bloke as a *'self-made billionaire'*.

Self. Made. Billionaire. And if you dare ask me what's wrong with that, I'm telling you, I'm going to blow my top. If *I* was on the radio right now, they'd have to play the *John on the Rhondda* theme tune while I cooled down.

Some people don't recognise that theme tune of mine. I'm sure that bloke on the news wouldn't. *When the Coal Comes from the Rhondda*. The old miners' song, taken up by football fans who've never been near a pit. And I'll come to the coal that came from the Rhondda, now just.

But let's get back to this 'self-made billionaire'. You were going to ask me, weren't you, before I scared you off: "A 'self-made billionaire'," you were going to say, "what's the problem with that?" Well, I reckon I'm just about calm enough now to give you an answer. 'Self-made billionaire'? There's only three things wrong with it.

First, whatever this bloke did, he didn't do it all by him*self*.

Second, he hasn't *made* anything of significance, not even his own self.

Third, there's no such thing as a *billionaire*, 'cos there's no such thing as a billion pounds.

'Self-made billionaire': wrong on all three counts. Happy now? Oh, don't tell me I've got to explain it to you. Alright then. I'd better take it one stage at a time, for the sake of my blood pressure. Why don't you whistle that theme tune of mine, whilst I compose myself?

'Self-made billionaire' by *John on the Rhondda* – Part 1: 'Self'
To be honest, I don't really know very much about this bloke, this 'self-made billionaire'. But let's assume he didn't *inherit* his money. That's usually the way people understand 'self-made'. But – did he teach himself to wash his own face? To get dressed in the morning? Did he learn how to read and write all by himself – or was it in a school where there were teachers, who'd been taught to read and write themselves, by other teachers?

Who built the school? Who cleaned it? Who bought the books? Who paid the teachers?

I don't think he did it all by himself, did he? And when he started work, on his first day, was he sitting there all by himself, talking to himself? No, pound to a penny, he was in an office. An office built by somebody, cleaned by somebody, and some people who'd been taught to read and write told him how to get started. Then he picked up a phone, a phone that was invented by somebody a *lot* clever than he was, and designed by somebody, and manufactured by somebody, and connected by somebody to a cable (made by somebody) that stretched all the way along a set of posts that were put up by somebody, so that he could talk to somebody (who was holding another phone, which had been connected by somebody and made by somebody) and ask them if they had enough money to buy something that somebody else had made and which he could send them in a van, which was designed by somebody, assembled by somebody, driven by somebody along a road built by lots of bodies, according to a plan drawn up by somebody who'd been taught to read and write and plan by teachers, who themselves... etc., etc. *That's how his fortune began.*

'Self-made billionaire' by *John on the Rhondda* – Part 2: 'Made'
Nobody makes a billion pounds for themselves by making things. That's obvious when you think about it. A billion is one thousand million. So let's say you could make something in an hour that you could sell for a clear profit of a thousand pounds. Tall order! To make a billion pounds, you'd need to sell a million of them. To make a million of them yourself, at an hour a piece – if you didn't stop to sleep or eat or do anything else – would take you 114 years. No, this 'self-made billionaire' didn't make anything himself – apart from money. He put together a deal, in which other people did the work, and he kept the profit. I'll tell you who *did* make a billion pounds by their own sweat and blood, though. Welsh miners. In a single year, 1913, they produced 57 million tons of coal, at least 10 billion pounds' worth at today's values. No wonder the first ever million-pound cheque is said to have been written in Cardiff's Coal Exchange. That's why I reckon my grandfather and thousands of colliers like him were Rhondda billionaires. They deserved to be, at any rate. But a billion pounds isn't all it's cracked up to be...

'Self-made billionaire' by *John on the Rhondda* – Part 3: 'Billionaire'
Got a fiver on you? Or any banknote? Take it out. Go on. Have a look at it. Carefully. See what it says in the small print? Put your glasses on if you need to. Get a magnifying glass. I'll tell you what's written on *my* five-pound note. There it is – I can just about make it out, right under the lovely flowing script that says 'Bank of England': "I promise to pay the bearer on demand the sum of five pounds".

What I'm holding isn't five pounds. It's only a promise to pay me five pounds, a promise made by the Bank's Chief Cashier, somebody called Victoria Cleland, if I can read her tiny, tiny signature on my fiver properly. But when I googled the Bank of England just now, it turns out Victoria left her job in 2018, and the Chief Cashier is now Sarah John – which might be handy for me, 'cos my mother's maiden name was John, so we may be related!

If I turn up at the Bank of England with this note and demand my five pounds, how would Sarah John pay me? With another note that says, "I promise to pay the bearer on demand the sum of five pounds"? And if all of us turned up, all at the same time, with all of our notes, demanding payment, you probably know from watching *Mary Poppins* what would happen. We wouldn't get our money, there'd be a run on the bank, and pretty soon afterwards the whole financial system would collapse.

Money, you see, is just a system of mutual trust. Or put another way, a con trick. "Money is the probably the most successful story ever told," said one wise man (Professor Yuval Noah Harari). "It has no objective value... but then you have these master storytellers: the big bankers, the finance ministers... they tell a very convincing story. 'Look at this piece of paper, it is actually worth 10 bananas'... and it works. Try doing that with a chimpanzee!"

So, a billionaire isn't somebody who's got a billion pounds in the bank. He's just somebody who trusts he's got a billion pounds in the bank. And who trusts that we all trust that he's got a billion pounds in the bank too. If we stopped trusting the bank, or stopped trusting him, I wonder what use all his lovely money would be then. The point is that money is a social contract, an agreement between two parties (and many more) that it's worth something. The next time you hear somebody boasting about 'my' money (or moaning about what the taxman is doing with it), it may be worth reminding them of that. If they keep it all to themselves, it isn't worth a penny.

I started this chapter by giving off about the idea of a 'self-made billionaire'. I seem to have proved that there's no such thing. What I do know is that my grandfather, 'Dai Clydach'/'Dai Budgie', in his long years of labour with his butties deep underground in Trehafod, sent hundreds of thousands of tons of the best Rhondda steam coal up to the surface, for other people to make fortunes selling – and that he ended his days with next to nothing in the bank. *Grôt a dime*, as he might have said in Welsh – literally 'fourpence ha'penny', but meaning the tiniest sum. In fact, Gransha didn't even earn enough for the banks to allow him the dignity of opening an account. There was an injustice in that. And it was certainly an injustice that his death certificate avoided any mention of the coal dust in his lungs that shortened his life; so his widow, my Nana, had no compensation when he died. But he and those other Rhondda billionaires he worked alongside were rich in ways that money can't account for.

So it does annoy me that people should glorify someone as a 'self-made billionaire', yes. And I'm livid that so many of those who have more than enough in the bank use their filthy lucre in ways intended to make sure that people like themselves, with more than their fair share of this world's wealth, get to keep it. I think that's an iniquity, and we should all work to end it. But I don't feel jealous of anyone. I had a grandfather, a Rhondda miner, who did an honest day's work and knew the proper value of everything. I had a grandmother, a Rhondda homemaker, who told me I was worth "all the tea in China". I may not have been, but to hear her say it was worth, yes, "all the tea in China" – and at least fourpence ha'penny more!

29

Shopping at the Kwop

YOU'VE CAUGHT ME on the hop here... I'm out shopping. And all without so much as talking to a shop assistant. Here I am scanning my own groceries... in Welsh. The things you can do nowadays!

The Welsh Government wants a million Welsh-speakers by 2050. It's official policy. I wonder if they're counting machines like this one, as well as people. *"Diolch am siopa yn y Coe-Op,"* it says – thanks for shopping where? The Coe-Op? It's the Kwop, or the Kop, mun. If you're speaking Welsh, talk tidy!

The Kwop. The Kop. One or the other. That's what it is. The definite article and *one* syllable, not two. That's what we call it in Penygraig, anyway. And in Penygraig, like lots of other Rhondda towns, the Kwop – or Kop – had a proud history. So let me tell you about it.

It's Saturday, 16 May 1891. Penygraig is a bustling new town, expanding rapidly in the shadow of Mid-Rhondda's coalpits, home to one of Wales's leading rugby clubs and to a splendid brass band all of its own. And there are shops and pubs and cafés and churches and chapels. But a new idea is about to take root here. In the Long Room of The Butcher's Arms – a famous meeting place for miners – a gathering is underway. The express purpose is *'to initiate the movement of starting a Co-operative Society'*. Not to start a Co-operative Society, mind you, but to *'initiate the movement of starting'* such a society.

If you're sensing some hesitation there, it's not surprising. A year or two earlier, a similar venture in Tonypandy had collapsed. A lot of investors had got their fingers burned. But us Penygraig people are made of stern stuff: the Penygraig Industrial Cooperative Society was duly constituted. Sums of £5, £10, even £20 were deposited as shares. Shop premises were bought from Moses Rowlands: a mine-owner as well as a shopkeeper, a big cheese in Penygraig. I don't know if he sold cheese, mind. But the Kwop was about to. Because that was the whole idea: to sell groceries and other essentials – clothes and boots and shoes and ironmongery, even – and to do that at competitive prices. But, and this was the crucial point, rather than the profit on the sales falling into the hands of a single owner (someone like Moses Rowlands) who was already rich enough to finance the business privately, it was the members of the Cooperative Society themselves who were to benefit from the profits accrued. They would get a *dividend*. Between them, they would own the business where they shopped, so they were perfectly entitled to share out the profits in whatever way they liked. And what they liked was sharing it amongst themselves. The 'Kwop Divi' had arrived in the Rhondda.

Local people liked this new idea. Business boomed. In its first trading quarter, ending on 31 December 1891, the balance sheet showed that the Penygraig Kwop had sold goods to the value of £1,722, 3 shillings and 6 pence. And the members got a dividend of three shillings for every pound they'd spent. Unlike those Tonypandy investors, who'd caught a cold, Penygraig had a divi that wasn't to be sneezed at.

All the same, the Society didn't really begin flourish until 1901, when it appointed a new manager, William Job, and a new Secretary, the splendidly named Martin Luther Thomas. Together they worked steadily to build a stronger Society, paying high dividends, opening a bakery, and new branches in Tonyrefail and Gilfach Goch, in Coed-ely and

Williamstown. In 1914, in Penygraig itself, 'more commodious and modern' premises were opened on Tylacelyn Road: the Society's flagship store. The grocery, drapery and furnishing departments took up a whole block of the street-front, and the name 'Penygraig Industrial Cooperative Society Ltd.' was proudly inscribed above the shop windows.

Just behind the new store, on Cross Street, the imposing office headquarters oversaw a whole retail empire. But it wasn't just about selling things. The Society played a crucial role in the social and cultural life of Penygraig. There were educational classes, grants for schooling and lectures for members and members' children. There were Cooperative choirs, Cooperative concerts, Cooperative *eisteddfodau*, Cooperative film shows. The Kop was said to be 'the busiest place in Penygraig', crowded daily with people not just shopping, but making dividend withdrawals and share capital deposits, using the savings bank, collecting tickets for hospital treatment, and taking advantage of a host of other services which the Society offered.

During the bitter strikes of 1910, 1921 and 1926, the Penygraig Cooperative nailed its colours to the mast. It supported the miners and their families with credit facilities to cover the lion's share of their weekly shopping bills, and grants which kept the wolf from the door. Donations rolled in from other Cooperative Societies, and the Society supplied ingredients for the miners' soup kitchens at cost price. And, in the run up to Christmas, members' children weren't forgotten.

When better times came around, the Penygraig Kwop prospered. When they counted it all up, in its first fifty years of trading, up until the Second World War, a staggering £8.8 million pounds was rung through the tills. It had paid out to its members – six thousand of them by then – dividends of £780,000. At today's values, you're talking the kind of money only a Russian oligarch has at his disposal.

Up the Rhondda!

My family – on my mother's side, anyway – were stalwart members of the Penygraig Society from its earliest days. My great-grandmother, known to all as Gua, was the wife of a craftsman, the local blacksmith, and when she went shopping, even in an institution as egalitarian and fair-spirited as the Kwop, I suppose she felt that that gave her a special status. I was always told that she would march into the store and, no matter how busy it was, how deep the queue at the counter, she would demand immediate service. No-one but William Job, the manager, was good enough to serve her. I don't suppose it made her very popular. I wonder what she'd make of being served by a machine.

My own early memories of going 'up the Kop' are all to do with how steep my little legs found the climb up Tylacelyn Road, and how heavy the bags of shopping were that I carried back down the road from the main store. By then, one of the senior managers in the Society was a Penygraig dignitary, Jackie Dawson Jones. *Mister* Dawson Jones always wore a bow tie, I remember, though I was never served by him. I obviously didn't have the pulling power of my great-grandmother. Thankfully, I never met him in his other official capacity either: he was a local JP.

Back home, a drawer in the sideboard was filled with Kwop books. I can see the covers now, a sickly beige, and inside the ledger of the family's purchases, handwritten, only the duplicate pages remaining, and the blue carbon sheet tucked at the back, bearing the imprint of what we'd spent, so that our dividend could be calculated.

A lot has happened to the Kop since then, in Penygraig, elsewhere in the Rhondda and across the whole country. The story of its changing ownership is too complicated to recount here and now. But I'm still shopping at the Kwop, and there's still a little dividend that comes back to me with every pound I spend, even if it's totted up electronically now when I scan my membership card at the till.

I can't help feeling, though, that something's been lost along the way – and not just the personal service that no machine can give you, no matter how quick and accurate it is. Not just that, but the whole cooperative idea and ideal. Back on its 50th anniversary in 1941, the Penygraig Industrial Cooperative Society could boast: *'It's our Society. Every brick, every pound in the bank belongs to us, all six thousand members.'* By combining their resources and their spending power, the pioneers of the Cooperative Movement had invented a splendid model – but it's now the exception rather than the rule. Perhaps it's time we considered why that is, why we've gone along with a system of retail therapy that allows a very few individuals to line their pockets with our pounds, even if we seem to be saving a few pennies along the way.

As I've said, I'm a huge admirer of the way Treorchy's high street has been revived as the home to quality independent shops owned by local people. Maybe for the inspirational people who've led *that* revival, there's further inspiration to be found in the history of the Kop, or the Kwop... or whatever you want to call it.

30

Ponty

I'M GOING TO Ponty this week, I am. There's exciting, isn't it? A trip to Pontypridd. It's market day! And all the shops will be open. Is it too early to be buying Christmas presents?

Pontypridd – originally *Pont-y-tŷ-pridd*, 'the bridge by the earthen house' – is famous for its Old Bridge, the Rocking Stone up on the Common, the Chain Works, and as the home of two men with the same name who composed a song that's still going strong a century and a half later, though it's known by another name now; and... as the hometown of another music man who changed his name and found global fame.

The fact is, Ponty has got a bit of a thing about names. Hang about, and I'll spell it out for you...

P. O. N. T. Y. P. R. I. D. D. Pontypridd. It's where Rhondda people go when we've got a tidy bit of shopping to do. I like to think of it as not in the Rhondda but of the Rhondda. It's where the River Rhondda meets the Taff, and that's why it needed a bridge. Originally, a succession of wooden bridges spanned the river, giving Ponty its name. But then a stonemason called William Edwards got to work. Depending how you look at it, he was either a genius of a bridge builder or a disaster waiting to happen. In 1756, at the fourth time of asking, he succeeded in replacing the last wooden bridge with what was, at the time, the longest single-span stone arch bridge in the world.

The reason it was the fourth attempt was, of course, that the first three all fell down. His touch of genius on the fourth try was to make three round holes in the stonework at each end of the bridge, reducing its weight and making sure that it stayed up. Honestly.

Unfortunately, almost as soon as it was finished, people started to complain about the shape of the bridge itself. William Edwards had designed it as a perfect segment of a circle, with an arch so steep that carts couldn't be pulled across it without rolling rapidly down the far side and crashing into the poor horses in front. All the same, from practically the moment the Old Bridge was put up, Pontypridd changed its name to Newbridge. And that's the way it stayed for a whole century, until the public got so fed up dragging the carts up and over the arch on chains that they paid for a flat bridge, the Victoria Bridge, to be put up next to the Old Bridge. So now that it had a new bridge, Newbridge became known as Pontypridd again. Are you following? No, it doesn't make much sense to me either.

Let me tell you about the Rocking Stone instead. And this time, instead of our stone bridge builder, William Edwards, I'm going to be talking about another stonemason, one who was called Edward Williams. William Edwards, Edward Williams... look, I know it's confusing, so to help us out, let's call this second chap... Iolo Morganwg. How about that? Strangely, as I've mentioned before, that's just what he called himself when he was being all bardic and Celtic and romantic. Which was most of the time. Wordsworth was doing much the same, in the same period. Well, maybe not so much the Celtic bit, though he did get as far as Tintern Abbey. Anyway, when Iolo Morganwg saw a big lump of rock sitting on top of Pontypridd Common, he said to himself, *"Ha! this must be a glacial boulder left over from the Ice Age."*

No. He didn't say that, to himself or to anyone else, no matter that that's what it really was. What he actually said, being all bardic and Celtic and romantic, was something like [adopts high-pitched bardic Celtic romantic voice],

"This must be a sacred stone consecrated by druids in ancient ceremonies dating way back to the dawn of Time. And now this is the moment, and we are the generation, destined to revive this age-old practice. This shall be called the Gathering Place of the Bards. The Gorsedd. And... I'll invent the Eisteddfod so that we can do it there as well."

And that, basically, is what happened. The National Eisteddfod, which is coming to Rhondda Cynon Taff in 2024, with its harps and flower-girls and swords and white-robed bards winning chairs and crowns – it all stems from a bloke staring at a stone on Ponty Common and being so proud and passionate about his Celtic roots that, when he couldn't find much actual historical evidence for these ancient Bardic ceremonies, he simply forged it. You couldn't make it up. Except, of course, that Iolo Morganwg did.

Let's move on. To the Chain Works. Thankfully, this bit of Ponty's story doesn't involve anyone called William or Edward. But it does feature a pair of Sams: Samuel Brown and his cousin Samuel Lenox. Brown Lenox & Co. Ltd. opened up in Pontypridd – or rather Newbridge – around about 1816. The factory quickly made its mark, supplying the ironwork for the Union Chain Bridge at Berwick on Tweed, now the oldest surviving vehicular chain bridge in the world. It opened more than two hundred years ago, in July 1820. From that date, Brown Lenox made the anchor chains for every Royal Navy ship right up until the First World War. And they did the same for fleets and fleets of cargo vessels and passenger ships, from Brunel's steamship the *Great Eastern* through to Cunard's *QE2*. My grandfather Tommy John, who spent most of his working life as the blacksmith at the Naval Colliery in Penygraig, plied his trade in Ponty's Chain Works during a downturn in the coal trade; and my Uncle Len, his son, did his apprenticeship as a welder there. It's nice to have family *links* to a distinguished piece of industrial history (*links – chains* – see what I did there?).

We've done the Williamses, the Edwardses and the Samuels – now it's time for the Jameses from Ponty.

James James – so musically talented they named him twice – was walking near his hometown one day in January 1856, when a very special tune came to him. He called it *'Glan Rhondda'* (the banks of the River Rhondda) because... well, that's where he was when the muse struck. Perhaps he'd used up his stock of originality on the melody itself. Indeed, that seems to be the case. Arriving home, he was clean out of inspiration: so he had to call upon his dad, Evan James, to think up words for his composition. And that's how the patriotic song we know as *'Hen Wlad Fy Nhadau'* came into being. By 1905, it had become recognised as our National Anthem. That year, it was the first anthem ever to be sung before an international sports fixture, when Wales took on – and beat – New Zealand's All Blacks in what was described as the rugby championship of the world.

By the way, if you're in danger of mixing up the father and son, Evan James was also known by the bardic name Ieuan ap Iago, whereas James James was also known by the bardic name Iago ap Ieuan. Does that help?

After all those Williamses, Edwardses, Samuels and Jameses, let's end with another Tommy. Not my grandfather, Tommy John, but Thomas Woodward, who strictly speaking comes from Treforest, though Pontypridd is usually acknowledged as his old hometown. He began his singing career as the frontman for a band called Tommy Scott and the Senators. And if you don't know what happened after that, you really haven't been paying attention. He made a name for himself. Clearly, as I've been trying to explain, in Pontypridd, it's not unusual.

31

Welsh Hills

A PHOTOGRAPH CAUGHT my eye this morning. I was browsing the internet, flicking through dozens of images, but this one meant something to me.

A fuzzy black-and-white picture, it was. Just a road, a typical terraced street on a hill, a few lampposts, the blurred side of a mountain in the distance. Hardly any distinguishing detail at all. It could have been one of a thousand streets anywhere in the Valleys, I suppose. But I knew instantly, without thought or calculation, where it was. Tylacelyn Road, Penygraig: *my* street.

How could I be so certain? It was the *angles* that gave the game away: the angles at which the houses were set against the rising road; the upright lampposts making angles against the sloping pavement; the angle at which the tilted road itself was set against the mountain in the background. Those precise angles were imprinted deep in my memory, so I could calibrate instinctively that – yes, this is Tylacelyn, my Tylacelyn.

I *knew* that road without thinking. I could do the same thing with plenty of others too. As I'm speaking to you now, if I close my eyes, I can picture to a fraction of a degree every gradient of every street in my home patch of Mid-Rhondda: the barely perceptible slant of Hendrecafn Road, the gentle slope of Hughes Street, the steep incline of Trinity Road, the daunting Matterhorn of Amos Hill, the Everest of Penygraig's Gilfach Road.

Try it for yourself with the streets you know best, and you'll see what I mean. If you grew up practically anywhere in hilly Wales, you've got a natural talent for geometry or trigonometry or whatever branch of mathematics it is that deals with lines and angles and the relationship between them. You can award yourself an A level in the subject right now – an honours degree, more like. Mind you, the credit's not really down to you: it's an automatic function of living somewhere like the Rhondda.

It's strange, I suppose, that it's a *mental* aptitude that we've gained from growing up in a place that's so hilly, rather than a physical one. And it has always seemed odd to me that most of the world's great middle-distance athletes and marathon runners come from Kenya and Ethiopia and Morocco, rather than from Hendrecafn Junior School. Imagine the times Kip Keino or Haile Gebrselassie would have posted if they'd trained every day by walking to school up Hill Street, like us.

Hill Street! It was rightly named. Short, but practically vertical. Back in the day, we used to play long pick-up games of football in the middle of any side-street we liked. There wasn't any traffic. One day, we decided to play on Hill Street. I can't imagine why. Maybe our favourite pitch down on Hughes Street had been blocked by some thoughtless motorist who'd decided they were entitled to park kerbside, like they owned the road! Didn't they know that it was our Wembley? Or maybe it was because Dilwyn Jenkins, the only one of our butties who lived on Hill Street, had finally snapped and demanded a home game for once. Anyway, we kicked off. Three-quarters of an hour later, at half-time, the ball had been in play for less than one minute all told. We'd spent the rest of the time taking it in turns to run all the way down to the bottom of the hill and halfway down Hughes Street to fetch that runaway football. The team kicking downhill was leading 23-0.

Playing football on Hill Street. It's experiences like that, I reckon, that give Rhondda people their attachment to fair play and fair shares for everyone. We *know* what happens when there isn't a level playing field. And living somewhere where everything is listing to one side or another *must* have an effect on our characters. Take my friends from Clydach. I've got a few, and they're not all unbalanced. But their journey home is like a Himalayan expedition. First, Court Street, curving upwards from Pandy Square, squeezing past the ramparts of the old Naval Club, then straightening into that implausible ascent, somehow hauling itself up to the plateau of Blaenclydach. And that's just Base Camp. Wern Street soars sharply upwards again to the summit of Clydach Vale. And the residents can climb all that without fixed ropes or oxygen. It's hardly surprising that everyone I know from up there comes at things from a bit of a tangent. It's not that *they* are out of kilter: it's the rest of the world that's all a bit flat and boring. Clydach people know that what makes life interesting is its ups-and-downs.

There's a new road that runs parallel to Court Street these days, part of the Tonypandy by-pass. Anyone who's driven it, from the junction down on the valley floor up to the roundabout by King George's Park, will appreciate what a crazy slant the highway is built at. No matter how hard you put your foot down, you'd better get ready to change gear: down, down, and down again, probably. You're practically in reverse. It's amazing to think that that slope once carried a railway – the colliery branch-line, scaling the Pwll yr Hebog Incline. It's famous amongst train enthusiasts. The railhead, of course, was higher still – up above Clydach, at the Cambrian Colliery. This stupendous feat of Victorian railway engineering was testament to the enormous value of the Black Diamond they'd found up there. Who would even contemplate building a rail track at such a pitch, unless untold wealth lay under the ground at its apex, just waiting to be exploited? According to one of my aunties, who habitually got such mathematical ratios the wrong way round, the gradient of the Pwll yr Hebog was 13 in 1. Walking up it, you suspected she might be right after all.

My father lived on top of a hill when he was a boy. It certainly played a part in forming *his* character. It gave him an extra helping of determination – what he would later call 'stickability'. You see, his house was on Top Trebanog Road, but he went to Infants School way, way down Cymmer Hill, which – as everybody who's ever travelled from Porth to Trebanog knows – might even top Court Street as the Rhondda's steepest, longest terrace. Dad was one of a small gang of Trebanog children who made their way down to school on foot every day – and they'd all come home for their dinner too, so they'd go down and back twice a day. The long climb home developed into a race, a twice-daily endurance marathon to see who could reach the top of the hill first. However hard he tried, Dad, being the youngest by a couple of years, could never come close to winning. No matter how much he'd huff and puff, some big kid always got there before him. But that's where the 'stickability' kicked in.

One fine morning, he promised himself that *this* was the day he'd finally come out on top. The moment the bell rang, he was on his feet, rushing out of the classroom. He was halfway to the school gate before he heard the rest of the children pouring out into the yard behind him. But he was off, pelting up the road, up the hill, as fast as his little legs could carry him. That climb was steep, so steep. He felt dizzy and sick. He'd been told that champion runners didn't look back to see how much of a lead they had. All they thought about was the finishing line. So he fixed his eyes on the hill ahead. And he was still in front. On and on he went, up and up and up, until finally he reached the top, and ran onwards on the flat towards his house, still struggling to catch his breath. When eventually he turned back to check, none of the others had even crested the brow of the hill yet. What a victory! What an achievement! Worthy of a gold medal at the Olympics. He fell in through the front door with hardly enough puff left to tell his mother about his great triumph.

"Mam! Mam! Mam!! *Mam!!!* I did it! Today… at last… I won the race!"

"Well, I'm not surprised," said his mother, calmly. "You've come home at playtime."

32
Rhondda Fach

I VENTURED INTO alien territory the other day. It was a risky mission, but someone had to do it. I boldly went to seek out new life and civilisation... in the Rhondda Fach! As you can gather in reading this, I've lived to tell the tale. So here's *John on the Rhondda*'s Guide to... 'The Other Valley'.

The Rhondda Fach. Let's start at the top. Maerdy: 'The Red Village', 'Little Moscow' – so called because years ago it was a stronghold of leading Communists from the South Wales Miners' Federation. Though one of my aunties – the same one who thought the Pwll yr Hebog Incline was 13 in 1 – was convinced it got its nickname because it's always so cold up there. It does look chilly, mind, in that iconic footage of the cheerless dawn at the end of the 1984–85 Strike, with the miners marching back to the pit, accompanied by the lodge banner and a brass band. The union tradition in Maerdy stood proud to the bitter end. In 1990, I took my son – he was just five at the time – to witness the last ever shift coming to the surface at the pithead. We have at home a piece of coal brought to the surface that day. The last shift in the last pit in the Rhondda. It felt like the end of an era. It *was* the end of era.

I'd filmed in Maerdy, not long after the Strike. I was making a documentary for the BBC's *Everyman* series about a motorcyclist who'd achieved some sort of enlightenment by riding literally all around the world. It took him four years. It was meant to be a film about travel and what it can teach the soul. I arranged an encounter between the biker and someone I'd got to know in Maerdy, a stalwart of the Maerdy Women's Support Group, those indomitable women who'd seen their men and their families through the hardship of the year-long strike. Barbara Williams was confined to a wheelchair and she'd seldom ventured far from Maerdy in her whole life, but from that single and singular perspective she'd developed a view of the world and gleaned more than enough wisdom to hold her own with any globe-trotter. As he rode out of Maerdy, my biker had to admit to the camera that, in their frank conversation, Barbara Williams had taught him far more than he'd had to offer her, for all that his heart had gleaned from those long days and nights on his epic road-trip.

My road takes me on to Ferndale. I filmed there in the 1980s too: with the Ferndale Home Improvement Service, a charity that, in those desperate Thatcherite times, was using the labour of otherwise unemployed locals to repair and redecorate old age pensioners' houses. They had a large-scale map on the office wall, showing every house in Ferndale and the neighbouring villages. They'd stuck a coloured drawing pin in each and every home they'd worked in. There were hundreds of pins, colour coded: a few yellow ones for the homes of elderly married couples; a couple of green pins for homes of widowed men; the rest red, for widowed women. The map was a sea of scarlet. The men, those old miners, had died of dust or disease long before their wives. The price of coal pinned to the wall for all to see.

My film showed how the Ferndale Home Improvement Service was doing more than DIY: it was fostering new relationships across the generations between the young workforce and the older occupants of the houses they were working on. It was *socialising* youngsters – youngsters who had every reason to be disaffected with the way the world was treating them, youngsters who'd scarcely spent time in any workplace, who hadn't had the chance to learn from older, wiser heads: something that used to occur naturally when there were apprenticeships on offer, down the mine or elsewhere in industry.

One of the workers on the 'scheme' – it was more or less compulsory for the jobless to take up the offer of working there – was slightly more mature than most. A real character, clearly a man of some intelligence and wit. If memory serves, he was called Brian. One morning during the shoot, whilst the crew were still setting up, I bumped into him coming out of the café on the Strand in Ferndale. He was midway through sharing an anecdote with one of the 'boys', and he finished it by quoting a Latin saying: *nemo mortalium omnibus horis sapit*, 'no mortal is at all times wise'. A working-class Ferndale man speaking Latin!

It was a classic Rhondda moment – like the one H V Morton had witnessed on that street corner in Tonypandy in the 1930s, when he heard two young miners discussing Einstein. It appealed strongly to my sense of how much ordinary Rhondda people respected education, how naturally smart they were, how well-read. I was desperate to capture it for the documentary. As soon as our camera was rolling, I asked Brian to repeat the phrase as though spontaneously. He did so, but rather shyly. It wasn't until I got into the cutting room that I discovered that it was the motto of the Royal Antediluvian Order of Buffaloes, the 'Buffs'. No doubt that was where Brian had picked it up. But it certainly made him look erudite in my documentary. As for me, the clever-clogs director, well, *nemo mortalium omnibus horis sapit!*

Onwards. A glance over the valley to Blaenllechau, home of my Porth County classmate Dai Leach, and down through Tylorstown, where another classmate, Michael Chapman, celebrated his eighteenth birthday with a legendary party. I was fortunate that in those days Porth County's catchment area was the whole of the Rhondda, both valleys. I got to know boys from 'The Other Valley' – and eventually girls too, when the Sixth Forms joined together. And I got to know what a 'doubler' was: fish and chips in Rhondda Fach parlance, at least in those days, but never called that in the Rhondda Fawr.

Nowadays, I suppose pupils in Ysgol Gymraeg y Cymer benefit from a similar experience – their school friendships must encompass both valleys too. For all the jokes and the rivalry, and the understandable feeling in the Rhondda Fach that it's the Rhondda Fawr that gets the better deal in terms of Council facilities and infrastructure, it goes without saying that there's much, much more that unites us. 'Together stronger', to steal the Wales football team's motto. That would be the Wales football team managed by a man from Tylorstown.

On again. We've no time to cross the valley to Stanleytown, but let's pause for a minute at Pontygwaith – 'the Bridge of the Works'. The name comes from an ironworks, a blast furnace said to have been built in the early sixteenth century, though by 1863 it was described as a 'shapeless ruin'. By the 1970s... I'm saying nothing! I was very fond of the place, and was a regular visitor to the home of one of those Sixth Form friends of mine, Elaine Pike. It was Elaine's father who – in later life and well beyond his hundredth birthday – was known to go for a walk, unaided, from the valley floor there in Pontygwaith all the way to the top of Penrhys. They breed them tough in the Rhondda Fach!

The road crosses the river now, and Wattstown is on this eastern bank, but we must press on. We're arriving at Ynyshir, the last village in the Rhondda Fach coming down from Maerdy – the first one if you're coming up from Porth. And this is why we're here. I want to call at The Workers Gallery. It's an exhibition space, a gift shop, a bookshop and a kind of mini-library all rolled into one. To my shame, I've never been here before and I'm not sure exactly where it is...

so I call at a corner shop on the main road in Ynyshir to ask directions. The shop assistant isn't content to tell me where to go, as it were: she insists on coming out from behind the counter and walking me up the road until she's absolutely sure that I can see my destination. A lovely instance of Rhondda neighbourliness – or kindness to a stranger, if you like: after all, I'm the one from 'The Other Valley' now. And the warm welcome continues in the Gallery itself from Gayle Rogers and Chris Williams, who run the place and are artists themselves.

Chris designed and made the Bardic Chair for the Cardiff National Eisteddfod in 2018, using a mixture of up-to-the-minute technology and traditional cabinet-making techniques. Gayle is an illustrator, cartoonist and graphic artist, who loves to research sport history, and is working on a graphic novel. She has a special interest in Duncan Edwards, the supremely talented Manchester United footballer and 'Busby Babe', who tragically died after being injured in the Munich Air Disaster in 1958. Gayle and Chris have kept the Gallery going through the pandemic and weathered storm damage to the building itself last winter. The Gallery is their pride and joy, and on this first brief visit there, I can sense the generosity of spirit that fills the place.

Something else is impressive about Gayle and Chris too: their unwillingness to compromise on the quality of the art they have on display. They simply won't exhibit the kind of cheap tat that might sell in volume, but won't challenge, intrigue or truly thrill anyone. It's a shining example of people doing something small-scale and local, but which can reach out and be a big inspiration in other people's lives and for their creativity. If you haven't been there, they'd love you to pay a visit. Entry is entirely free.

So that's my guide to the Rhondda Fach – home of artists and of that powerhouse of working-class music, the Pendyrus Male Choir, birthplace of legends like actor Stanley Baker and rugby player John Bevan, filming location for *Stella* (and for some of my documentaries!). It may be the smaller valley, the little Rhondda, but *Fach* can be also term of endearment – so Rhondda Fach would mean something like 'dear old Rhondda'. And that's a way to think about it that we can all sign up to, wherever we're from.

33

Treorchy: Higher and Higher

JUST WHEN I thought I couldn't love what's happening on Treorchy's high street any better, they've come up with a promo that really knocks my socks off. It takes us on a whistle-stop video tour that challenges – head on – the assumption that the era of vibrant local shops is over and done, and that you can get it all cheaper online these days. *No!*, assert the young, smart presenters, in their unashamedly expressive local accents, Treorchy is *different*. It's a UK Champion high street, for one thing, and home to 35 spanking *new* businesses which have sprung up amidst the old favourites, bucking the trend that's decimated shopping centres in more affluent localities. These are genuine local enterprises, some of them with world-class goods to sell, and many offering service in Welsh as well as English.

Treorchy seemed a world away when I was a nipper, even though I was brought up only half a dozen miles away, but it features large in my earliest memories. As a toddler, I used to take a monthly trip there with my grandmother. She had to go all the way up the valley to pay money in at an insurance agent's office opposite The Stag. Of course, this was long, long before the days of electronic bank transfers. The wife of a collier – my Gransha, the faceworker at Lewis Merthyr Colliery – she didn't have a bank account anyway. So to keep a policy paid up, or pay off what was effectively a mortgage, I'm not sure which, Nana had to turn up in person and deposit cash. We'd travel up from Tonypandy together on the bus, her clutching her navy handbag, me with my sky-blue toy steering wheel, top deck, front seat, driving the bus myself and counting off every stop along the way... *Partridge Square, Old Penrhys, Carter's Corner* and so on. That's how I got my love of buses, their routes and timetables. Me and my magic steering wheel. I'm still a sucker for public transport, but these days I prefer to take the train up to Treorchy – it gives you a slightly different perspective on the valley, and it's always good to look at the familiar with fresh eyes.

Years ago, a branch of our family lived in Treorchy, and my Mam's mother is buried in Treorchy cemetery, not far from that long row of graves which seem to belong exclusively to publicans. So over the years I've not been a stranger to Treorchy. And there are things about the town I've always loved, such as the Treorchy Male Choir. As I've mentioned (proudly!), one of my films had a premiere in Treorchy's stunning hall of working-class culture, the Park and Dare. My favourite Rhondda band, Peruvian Hipsters, were a bunch of Treorchy reprobates. And – again, as I've already declared – one of my very best friends and colleagues, Phil George, grew up in Dumfries Street. Number 47. Despite all of this – or perhaps because of the rivalry that makes the best friends josh each other – I never let Phil get away with bigging up his hometown over my patch, Mid-Rhondda. Penygraig and Tonypandy's roads and *gwlis* and back-lanes, the ones I knew best when I was growing up, are still the ones I love to champion whenever I can. So I can't be accused of any bias when I say that these days – in terms of its shopping centre, anyway – it's clear that Treorchy is streets ahead.

I'm reluctant to portray myself as any kind of prophet, but it's half a decade and more since I began to sense that something special was going on on Treorchy's high street. I'd get off the train and head straight to the High Street Social for a frothy coffee. Then a stroll, window-shopping, up to Cyril the butcher's. Cyril Morris is a Treorchy institution, and since my friend Phil George was now a Treorchy exile, I knew that I'd be in his good books for weeks if I brought him back as a small present a few of Cyril's choice faggots.

But even on those short walks, I could tell that something was up. Something good. A stirring in the heart of the community, cafés full of gossiping shoppers, footfall noticeably on the increase, a variety of new, young businesses opening – and not just the usual suspects. It was just before the first lockdown that all this led to Treorchy high street being crowned the UK's best. In the prestigious Great British High Street Awards for 2019, Treorchy was named 'High Street of the Year'. It was commended not just for the shops, but for its community-led year-round cultural events – an outdoor cinema, an arts festival and an annual Christmas Parade. All of these seemingly peripheral activities were actually central to generating the increasing footfall I'd noticed. The training and support that was being offered to local businesses also caught the judges' eyes. It was the second year in a row that a high street in Wales claimed the top prize, following Crickhowell's triumph in the Awards for 2018. I'm sure that that victory was well-deserved too, but I can't help thinking that Treorchy's was the more impressive, given the economic and geographical challenges the Rhondda faces.

Challenges, did I say? Adrian Emmett sees them as opportunities. Though he'd be the first to share the credit with others, he's the galvanising force behind much of the transformation in Treorchy. Adrian owns The Lion pub, which nestles right at the heart of the shopping Mecca, and which has just scooped a UK-wide gong of its own: the 'Community Hero' award in a competition dubbed the 'Oscars' of the British pub industry.

As Chair of Treorchy's Chamber of Trade, Adrian Emmett has grown its membership from 30 to 120. And he *does* regard challenges as opportunities. When The Lion had to close during lockdown, he turned the pavement space outside the shuttered front door into an open-air fruit and veg market – and, when the pandemic regulations eased, that morphed into Green Valley, a zero-waste supermarket selling fresh food of real quality, much of it produced locally. Green Valley has also, incidentally, sold more copies than any other single outlet of my book, *The Great Welsh Auntie Novel*. A tender love story, with a magical realist twist, selling alongside the caulis and carrots: where but in Treorchy?

There's a phrase that's used when we give a lot of public attention and approval to someone – we 'lionise' them. Well, the owner of The Lion doesn't need me or anyone else to lionise him. The achievements of Treorchy's high street speak for themselves. And I think they genuinely are shared achievements, communal achievements – they belong to everyone in the town, and the whole area. And now, Adrian Emmett and brilliant colleagues like Angharad Walters, the founder of *Cymru Wrth Galon/All Things Wales*, want to press on to another level again. Under the umbrella of *'Love Treorchy'* they've not only created that stunning video, but they've also taken a scientific approach – surveying visitors and developing ambitious new plans that appeal to them. The survey established that Treorchy already has a fantastic 91% overall approval rating. And the research suggests that the new projects – which include pushing for an outdoor community space, broadening what's on at the Park and Dare, and pioneering the concept of a whole shopping centre that's 'smart', in the digital way your 'smart TV' operates – will boost visitor numbers further, with a positive knock-on effect for local shops and businesses, creating a virtuous upwards spiral of growth and prosperity for the whole community.

'Ni yw Treorci' / *'Treorchy – that's us'*: it's a great strapline and a wonderful good-news story in and of itself. But it can also serve as a model and an inspiration to the whole valley.

There's a lot of talk these days about 'levelling up'. Well, I think 'levelling up' shouldn't be something that's done *for* us, or *to* us – it should be something we do for ourselves, and not just levelling up to some notional national average, but going further, with the kind of ambition that's always characterised the Rhondda. Treorchy is a place where the high street went higher – and higher. So for the whole valley, let's say it: *'Ni yw'r Rhondda'* – together we can soar to even loftier heights.

34

Fair Play

IT'S QUIZ TIME again with *John on the Rhondda*. And here's your starter for 10...

In which sport would you find the Porth Whites taking on the Tonypandy Reds, and the Treorchy Blacks playing the Ferndale Navys?

Well, if *you* don't know the answer – and it's an inspiring one – I reckon there are at least eleven hundred people in the Rhondda who do. Yes, 1,100 at the very least. They're aged from 4 to 65. And they all belong to the same gender.

Rhondda is sports mad. Always has been. Back before the pandemic hit, someone who knows about these things started counting the number of teams in the Rhondda in three of our leading sports, taking all the age-groups into account as well as senior players. There were 11 cricket teams, 97 football teams and 109 rugby teams. Pretty amazing stats, eh?

But those figures don't tell the whole story. You see, those were the numbers of *male* teams in those sports. The picture for *female* teams was a bit different. Just 10 female football teams, 6 female rugby teams and no opportunities at all if you were a batter, bowler, fielder or wicketkeeper who just happened to be female. So, overall, in these three major sports there were only 16 female teams, as opposed to 217 male teams. For Rhondda women, it seems, it's just not cricket. Or much football. Or rugby.

In case you're wondering, the person who compiled those statistics was... a man: Lawrie Davies, founder of Rhondda

Netball. Lawrie's point is that female sport is trapped in a kind of negative loop. Women and girls are less likely to play sport because they don't have teams to play in or against; and because the teams don't exist, neither do the facilities; and because the facilities don't exist, women and girls are less likely to play sport.

But Lawrie Davies wasn't content just to let this vicious circle go round and round forever, strangling the potential he saw. He wanted to cut through, to change the way people think, to raise aspirations and expectations. He had a *vision* for what netball could do for Rhondda girls and women. And perhaps that's not surprising. Lawrie, you see, is the son of someone you've already met in this book: Phil Davies, the marketing guru who helped Treorchy's rugby 'Dream' to become a reality back in the 1990s. Now, a generation later, it's Lawrie's turn to make his mark on the Rhondda's sporting landscape. And he's begun to do just that – big time!

Established just a few years ago in 2016, Rhondda Netball has rapidly become the biggest female sports initiative in Wales. Every week, eleven hundred girls and women take part, in centres up and down the Rhondda. And yes – you've guessed it – netball is the answer to my quiz question about the sport played by those multicoloured Rhondda township teams. They're part of the Rhondda Cynon Taf Netball League, which boasts eight divisions across five age-groups. And on top of all that, at an elite level, the Rhondda Rockets represent the best of our valleys – and represent us *with distinction*, in competitive action against teams from right across south Wales. In 2021/22, both the Rhondda Rockets Under 11s and Under 12s won their respective leagues, while the Under 18s took the honours in their division, and the senior Rhondda Rockets team triumphed as overall champions of the A470 Netball League.

Of course, organising and administering, coaching and kitting out so many teams and players is more than a one-man task. Lawrie Davies is joined in Rhondda Netball's senior management team by Jody Barnes and Jessica Sutton, who double up as star players for the Rhondda Rockets. Credit must also go to the brilliant all-female team of leaders and coaches working at a community level in both the Rhondda Fach and the Rhondda Fawr.

It's a fully professional set-up, and it needs to be. The mantra is: 'With volunteers, you can build bungalows – but it takes professionals to construct skyscrapers.' And Rhondda Netball's ambition *is* sky high. It's much more than sport, they say. They're already making a massive social impact, creating opportunities for girls and women, fighting gender inequality. It's about social inclusion, improving mental health and emotional well-being, as well as encouraging participants to live active, healthy lives. As Tonypandy – and West End – singing star Sophie Evans says, "It's wonderful to see the positive impact Rhondda Netball is having, not only in giving young girls in the Rhondda more opportunities in sport, but also giving each girl involved a real sense of belonging, which is so important in raising their self-worth and self-esteem."

Judging by the response they get from the mams and dads of the girls involved, Rhondda Netball is certainly delivering on its mission. You can see it, in comment after grateful comment, set out in their Rhondda Netball brochures. The brochures are beautiful, by the way – almost works of art in themselves, full of glossy colour photos of the players in action and details of their exploits on court. The brochures speak of an organisation that's determined to produce quality in everything that it does. But those comments! One mam swears that "It's given a massive boost to my daughter's all-round self-confidence. She lives and breathes Rhondda Netball." And here are four more mothers' testimonials: "My daughter's attitude is so much more positive all around." "You can see her skills and confidence growing all the time."

"Her schoolteacher has noticed the difference in her too."
"You inspire her."

Perhaps my favourite quote is from the delighted mam who posted on Facebook a photo of her tiny, smiling daughter after a match, with the simple comment: "Look at her face, mun. She has loved every minute of taking part. Thank you, Rhondda Netball."

The brilliant Rhondda journalist and broadcaster Carolyn Hitt has observed that: "There's still so much work to be done in the 21st century to ensure women and girls are better represented across the spectrum of sport." And Rhondda Netball itself – for all the noteworthy achievements in its brief existence – faces challenges of its own if it's to realise its full potential.

Up till now, they've played in school halls and sports centres: places which have many other competing demands on their use. Lawrie Davies is adamant that Rhondda Netball needs a dedicated three-court venue of their own: without one, they won't be able to grow further and deliver on the stellar expectations that their players now have. They've always been able to stand financially on their own two feet, but in these days of intolerable pressures on family budgets, the question of facilities and the support of funding bodies is crucial.

So right now, Rhondda Netball is getting together its case for a fairer share of what's always been male-dominated sports funding. Fair play is all they're asking for, and to back up their argument they've got a battery of statistics which show how unbalanced the current provision of facilities is between male and female sport.

But, potentially, they've got something else too, something even more persuasive in the minds of the guardians of the public purse: parent power, the support of all those hundreds of mams and dads who *know* the huge difference the discipline and camaraderie of playing netball has made to their daughters. Stand by! If *they* start to make their voices heard, there could be a *lot* of noise.

Will they succeed, and take netball in the Rhondda 'rocketing' up to another level again? It won't be a slam-dunk. But then, if it was easy, anyone could do it. My money's on Rhondda Netball: after all, when they take aim, it's a fair bet they're going to hit the target.

35
Black Tips and Pyramids

It was a helicopter we went up in – me and the camera crew, and Jason Mohammad, the presenter of the TV series we were making about life amongst the world's highest mountains. Up we flew, up above the trendy ski resort of Zermatt, up and up again, until there was nothing to see but the elemental grandeur of 4000m-high snow-capped Alps, and the age-old Gorner Glacier beneath them, frozen even in high summer. And when I spotted it, in the distance – the distinctive shape of the Matterhorn, a massive pyramid dominating the horizon – it was then that I turned to our Swiss pilot and told him something he couldn't possibly have understood: "*Duw!*" I said, "It's just like the Rhondda!"

What on earth did I mean? Comparing his Swiss Alps to the Rhondda: had I gone crazy? Well, I must admit, I *was* a bit light-headed. The altitude. That dizzy ride in the chopper. All those mountain vistas – vast, majestic, breathtaking. But there was *some* logic in my madness, if I say so myself. I'd like to explain it properly; but first, let me tell you a bit more about why we were flying so high, and about the daredevil we were going to interview. Sam Anthamatten is a star of free-skiing. It's the ultimate modern sport: an extreme contest between man and mountain. We had spectacular high-definition footage, filmed from helicopters and drones, of Sam skiing at maximum velocity, off-piste, on the brink of impossible mountain edges and Alpine cornices, leaping off precipices to land on pristine snow with no waymarks, and then hurtling on down, down, down, testing to the utmost how steep a skiing line can get before it becomes an uncontrollable, disastrous fall.

"In my eyes, everything happens in slow-motion," Sam told us. "I have to make many, many decisions every second, but I make them very quickly. The biggest challenge is to push yourself to the limit. If I said I'm not a 'thrill-seeker', I'd be lying to myself."

We set up for the interview. To get the mountain range perfectly in shot over Sam's shoulder, we had to move him very, very slightly from where he was standing. Helpfully, Jason reached out to ease Sam's shoulder the last inch or so into the precise angle we needed. Sam was slight figure, trim, at least six inches shorter than Jason. But Jason told me afterwards that there was no 'give' at all when he pushed to make that final adjustment. Sam was perfectly poised, perfectly balanced, rock-solid in his stance. His physique, honed by his Alpine exploits, was as unyielding as the Matterhorn.

"I grew up in Zermatt," he told Jason on camera. "It's surrounded by Alps. You're *impelled* to go up the mountains, you're drawn to them. They made me who I am. Mountains aren't just part of my life, they *are* my life."

His words reminded me again of my upbringing in the Rhondda, of my own love of the steep upland terrain where I was reared. Behind Sam, the Matterhorn's distinctive white outline became for me the Black Tip, the pyramid of colliery waste above Mid-Rhondda, as I'd seen it covered in snow in the harsh winters of my boyhood. Like Sam, I was a son of the mountains, and though I'm pretty much the polar opposite of a world-class athlete, I too had memories of death-defying descents. On summer days, as nippers, we'd take cardboard boxes up to the top of the Black Tip, and we'd toboggan back down, helter-skelter. It wasn't quite free-skiing, but to us, it felt just as scary.

There's a photo I found of the Black Tip, taken in the 1960s, I suppose: a black-and-white image, taken on a long lens from the opposite side of the valley, from near Maes yr Haf, on Brithweunydd Road in Trealaw. The line of houses in the foreground leads the eye back across the *cwm* to where the Tip towers above Tonypandy. What's striking – it's truly alarming, to be honest – is that the foreshortening of the camera shot reveals dramatically how that massive black pyramid looms over Hendrecafn, my old junior school. It's impossible not to think of another junior school, two valleys away, in Aberfan. The 116 children who died in that terrible, terrible disaster in 1966 were of an age with me and my schoolfriends in Hendrecafn.

The people of Aberfan had to battle to get what was left of their coal tips removed. A Disaster Fund had been set up as a charity for public donations to support the bereaved. Shamefully, the Labour Government in Westminster raided it – to pay for the tips' removal.

In Mid-Rhondda, our Black Tip was eventually landscaped into the mountain, but every Rhondda pit had a waste tip, and many of them remain on our hillsides to this day. Most of them are grassed over now, and harmless-looking. But if they absorb too much rainwater or groundwater, some still have the potential to become sudden, deadly, fast-flowing rivers of slurry. Just a couple of years ago, in Tylorstown, heavy storms caused a landslide that sent 60,000 tonnes of spoil from a coal tip down Llanwonno mountain, causing massive disruption and huge anxiety to local residents.

Afterwards, news reports revealed that there are as many as 327 disused tips in Wales officially classed as 'higher risk'. The Welsh Government has said that increased rainfall due to climate change means that 'hundreds of millions of pounds' is needed to make the coal tips safe for good. It sounds like a lot of money, certainly beyond what the Welsh Government could readily afford in any given year – and of course it *is* a huge sum compared to anything you and I might have in the bank, compared to anything any individual might possess, unless they'd been made obscenely wealthy off the backs of other people's labour. But it's a drop in the ocean compared to what we know the UK Government can lay its hands on when it needs to – compared to the billions, for instance, that seem to have been wasted in the first few months of the pandemic on technology projects which were so badly mismanaged.

'Clear South Wales' Coal Tips' is a community-based group calling for action to make the tips safe, and for the Welsh Government to publish the list of those at risk. Reassurance is badly needed. Phil Thomas, who lives in Ynyshir, fears that he and his young family are living below one of them. Every time it rains, he says, he worries. "What do we do if something starts pouring down the hill? We've got no chance." He's pushed for publication of the full list of hazardous sites. I suppose it's understandable that the authorities want to be absolutely certain of the facts before raising public alarm, but all the same...

After Aberfan, it must have appeared reasonable to some powerful people to use the Disaster Fund to remove the tips. Half a century later, it seems incomprehensibly inhumane. I believe that it won't be that far into the future until it will seem just as incomprehensible that Britain, which was fuelled and enriched by our coal so handsomely and for so long, pretends it can't afford to restore our landscape, our mountains to what they were before they were despoiled by industry: safe places of spotless natural beauty.

I began this piece with a filming trip to the Alps, and a mountain shaped like a pyramid. I seem to have strayed a long way from there. Let me end with another foreign filming location which Jason Mohammad and I were privileged to visit together. The Step Pyramid in Saqqara has for decades being collapsing in on itself. Jason and I documented the restoration work – undertaken, believe it or not, by a firm of Welsh engineers. It was a magical – if rather anxious – experience, crawling through dusty, disintegrating tunnels which were four and a half thousand years old, to reach, at last, the king's burial chamber. The Pyramids of Egypt are wonders of the world, glorious human achievements – but ultimately, of course, they are memorials: reminders of mortality. Let's not leave it until more lives are lost before we deal with *our* pyramids of coal waste.

36

Our Field of Dreams

> In 1910, this is a modern stadium – with a rugby pitch, a grandstand, a running and cycling track. And for local people, it's a highly charged space – here they can play out their sporting dreams and ambitions at the highest level. It's a Field of Dreams where they can challenge the world.

THOSE ARE THE words of the late and much-lamented Eddie Butler, speaking in a BBC film I made back in 2010 to mark the centenary of the Tonypandy Riots. But do you know which ground he was talking about? Here's another clue from Eddie and that film script:

> By coming to this very same spot for their mass meetings, the miners of Mid-Rhondda are also laying down their challenge to the wider world.

The playing field Eddie was talking about is the Mid-Rhondda Athletic Ground. Or as we used to call it, with typical Rhondda bluntness, 'Mid'. Others know it as 'The Mid', or 'The Track'. Whatever you call it, Eddie Butler was right to say that, in holding their mass meetings there during the Cambrian Combine Dispute that led to the Tonypandy Riots in 1910, the 12,000 Mid-Rhondda miners were challenging the world, just like their elite sporting teams did.

And if you think that sounds a bit overblown – consider what went on in that stadium in 1908, just two years before the Riots.

In April 1908, the first-ever rugby league international between Wales and England was played there – Wales won 35-18, by the way. Then, on successive weekends that autumn, huge crowds paid handsome gate money to watch two epic contests featuring local teams – first Penygraig in rugby union, then Mid-Rhondda in professional rugby league. And in both cases, the visiting opponents had travelled to play on 'The Mid' from about as far anyone can on this planet – they were the full Australian national teams. Here's Eddie again, from the film:

> Penygraig v Australia may sound a little strange to the ear of a modern rugby commentator, but a hundred years ago, we were in the first Golden Era of Welsh rugby – and it was a natural match. The vanguard of modern Wales wanted to test itself against the best in the world.

After the First World War, it was the turn of soccer to take over the ground. I remember my grandfather telling me about the 'Mush', as they were called – Mid-Rhondda FC, a professional football team who took on the likes of Derby County, Aston Villa and Tottenham Hotspur. Glory days!

50 years later, I had my own moment of sporting glory on the Mid-Rhondda Athletic Ground. I wasn't a sporty child. I never got near being picked for our Hendrecafn Junior School soccer team, with its stars like prolific striker Paul Edwards and overlapping full-back Robbie Rees – 10 years old and 10 years ahead of his time. And when it came to athletics, Dai Michael could sprint from one end of Hughes Street to the other before I'd crossed it from side to side. So the only time I ever featured in the green vest and black shorts of Hendrecafn at the Annual Sports Day up on the Mid-Rhondda Field was as a member of the mixed-gender tunnel ball team. Tunnel ball? It's kind of gentle relay race, where you have to throw a football between your own legs and down the 'tunnel' of your teammates' spreadeagled lower limbs to the athlete at

the far end, who then runs to the front and does the same. It's unlikely ever to be recognised as an Olympic sport, I'll admit. But the points at stake *mattered* to us. The Sports Day was the biggest event in the junior schools' calendar, pitting Hendrecafn against our local rivals Tai, Alaw, Cwmclydach, Pontrhondda and a clutch of others. It was a huge occasion. And we were doing so well in the tunnel ball, neck-and-neck with Williamstown and the Catholic School… until I let the ball hit my leg, and it bounced away – the wrong way – out of the tunnel and out of reach, disqualifying us.

But I wasn't to be denied my moment of Mid-Rhondda Magic. Because it wasn't just on Sports Day and in organised inter-school football matches that we played on 'The Mid'. We made use of it all year round in our unofficial pick-up games of soccer, rugby and cricket. We were used to playing football in the side streets of Penygraig, even (as I've said) on Hill Street, which was more like mountaineering than soccer. But 'The Mid' was a different class of pitch. Instead of tarmac, it had grass! And it *was* a level playing field!

So after school some days, once we were sure that 'Jack', the fierce groundsman, had gone home for the evening, we'd head up to this Field of Dreams: up past the tumps, across the brook and the Incline, the derelict tramway that used to carry waste from the Naval Colliery up to the Black Tip above Mid-Rhondda. The Ground itself was shut to the public, the gates at the Ely Street end locked and the perimeter guarded by a continuous line of upright metal railings, too high for any child to climb. But just at their lowest point, by the side of the Incline, a pair of the railings been prised apart – just enough so that by turning sideways we could squeeze through the gap. Then all that lovely neatly mown grass was ours!

I remember we used to go up there on Good Friday, the first day of the Easter holidays, with hot cross buns for a picnic. We'd play to our hearts' content, or at least until we wore ourselves out. Easter marked the crossover between winter sports and the cricket season. And it was cricket that gave me my Magic Moment. I was 10. The game – Hughes Street vs. Mikado Street – isn't recorded in Wisden or any of the annals of cricket, but to us it was as important and as tense as any Test match. And the bowling every bit as fierce. The two teams were big boys, most of them three or four years older than me. Tony Stevens captained Hughes Street, I think, and maybe it was John Long who skippered Mikado. Hughes Street were short of a player, and because I'd brought along that bat that my Uncle Len had given me, I was pressed into service: a non-bowling number 11, only to be called upon if all the other batters were out. Well, that's what happened: nine others back in the pavilion – well, back in the rusty, open Mid-Rhondda grandstand – and big Gary Dodds stranded at the bowler's end. As I strode out to join him, shaking with nerves, there was an edgy silence, *almost* like the one in that famous poem by Sir Henry Newbolt:

> There's a breathless hush in the Close to-night –
> Ten to make and the match to win –
> A bumping pitch and a blinding light,
> An hour to play and the last man in.

We had only seven to make, not ten. But I don't think I'd ever faced a proper, hard cricket ball before – us nippers used to play with tennis or sponge balls. All the same, I had Uncle Len's bat, and that was my secret weapon. As I've explained, Len was a stalwart follower of Glamorgan, and – alongside Gary Sobers's signature – he'd got one of his local heroes to sign the back of the bat. Jeff Jones wasn't much of a batter. He was an ace fast bowler, but definitely a number 11 when it came to batting, just like me. I knew, though – *of course I did! Len had never stopped talking about it!* – that that winter, Jeff Jones, the last man in, had bravely batted out the final over of a Test match against the fearsome fast-bowling of the West Indies, thereby drawing the game and winning the series. He was my talisman, his autograph my protection against the missile that was about to come speeding my way. And it worked. Though my teeth were chattering, my grasp was steady. I played cautiously, correctly, forward. I was just a fraction awry picking out the line of the delivery. The ball spun off the edge of Uncle Len's bat, past the despairing dive of slip, and we scampered home for a single. Gary Dodds smashed the next ball halfway to Llwynypia for a six, and Hughes Street won the game! I was a hero. One not out, the bravest and best innings ever played on the Mid-Rhondda Athletic Ground.

In recent years, 'The Mid' has got into a sad state of disrepair. There was a danger that it might disappear from the landscape of Mid-Rhondda altogether: the Council, under financial pressure, had announced a plan to sell off the long-neglected ground, giving developers the option of building so-called 'low-density housing' there. Alarm bells rang in Tonypandy. This was *our* space, people realised, *our shared space* with its special history – a precious green space in a highly built-up area. Thankfully, a local campaign got going, a campaign to secure 'The Mid' and open it up as a resource for everyone in Mid-Rhondda, to make it a vibrant home again for sport and all sorts of activities, where the whole community could come together.

The 'Save the Mid-Rhondda Athletic Field' Campaign gathered mass popular support. Articulate, community-minded local residents like Stuart Smith, Phil Rowlands, John Charles and the late, dearly loved Paul Nagle took up the cudgels. For a long time, it seemed as though they were fighting a David-against-Goliath battle. Housing developers have deep pockets. They're used to competitive tenders, to compiling fully costed business plans, to estimating, detailing and justifying things like capital and revenue costs, just as the Council were demanding. But the campaigners had something more telling than that: they had heart. And they weren't going to give up...

In the end, they've been able to secure a commitment from the Council that *no* housing development will take place there after all. There's a new recognition in government – local and national – that welcoming green spaces offer enduring benefits to the wellbeing of both young and old. Enhancing the quality of daily life is a priority which can outweigh short-term financial gain. And rightly so.

So 'The Mid' will remain in Council hands, freely accessible to the public. Remedial work and improvements have begun, and in the long term, the hope is to restore the playing surface and to construct a 'heritage trail' around the pitch, celebrating its famous history. Once again it will properly belong to those who most cherish it, and who most need it.

Speaking to the campaigners about what they've achieved has gladdened my heart, some comfort in troubled times. In the grand scheme of things, it's a small victory. But we are where we are, and we can only do what we can do. Every time a David stands up against a Goliath, every time good people fight against all the odds, for what's right and true and just and fair and lovely, that *matters*. It matters in its own right, and also for the encouragement it gives to others.

Safeguarding 'The Mid' as a green outdoor space for future generations in Tonypandy has been described as a triumph of people power. It means so much to so many – that's evident in the hundreds of comments and 'likes' posted on social media as the news broke. The good guys won. It doesn't always go that way, but let's be thankful for the times it does, and for the gumption of those who saw it through.

37

The Record Shop

CAN YOU PICTURE it: the first LP you ever bought?

If you're the same dap as me, born in the late 1950s, your teenage taste in music was probably formed by watching *Top of the Pops*, and by tuning in to 'wonderful' Radio 1 on 247. Or, if you'd been clued in by cool and trendy friends, by listening to a pirate station like Radio Caroline in your bedroom at night. And the music your friends rated was crucial in deciding your taste too. Not that I'm suggesting you didn't have a mind of your own. I expect you already had a collection of singles, of 45-rpm discs, acquired when you first began to get pocket-money: chart hits that you played on the family's record player. Maybe your parents – if they were a lot more 'hip' and sophisticated than my Mam and Dad – had invested in a *stereo* system. And now... you were ready to graduate to your first proper grown-up choice: an *album*, a 12-inch long-playing record pressed onto black vinyl, all packaged up in a gatefold cover, a *sleeve*, adorned with the band's name and some snazzy artwork, and just waiting to delight and surprise you – once you'd switched speeds to 33 revolutions per minute. Two whole sides of tracks: 8, 10, 12 of them!

So, what was it, that first LP of yours? Something you'd be ashamed to admit to these days? Or a classic that still defines your taste all these years later? I can remember the first LP I ever bought, and precisely where. And I'll tell you about it – now just...

John Geraint

I'm moving house for the first time in 25 years, so I've had to decide what to do with my record collection. The scratchy vibe of vinyl has become trendy again: authentic analogue audio, as opposed to the antiseptic perfection of digital downloads. My collection amounts to a couple of hundred discs altogether, most of them recorded half a century ago; but we're *downsizing* – I think that's the term – so I've been 'encouraged' to jettison anything that's simply taking up space. Gritting my teeth, I managed to sift out as many as 40 or 50 records, ones that (if I'm being totally honest) scarcely get played any more, from one year to the next. I took them to that stall upstairs in Cardiff Market where they stock vintage discs, and I'm proud to say there wasn't a single album that they weren't eager to buy from me. Taste, you see: if you've got it, you've got it! And by the time I was buying LPs, I had it. Even if I say so myself. I've got to admit, though, that I was pretty late to whole pop and rock scene.

When I was a boy, we lived with my grandparents – our house in Tylacelyn Road, Penygraig had been bought, brand new, by my great-grandfather Robert John for the princely sum of £300 in 1903. Hardly anything in the house seemed to have changed since back then. It was gloomy, with varnished sideboards, coal scuttles and bible-black Bibles. The place suited a generation in the last decades of their lives, not the first. Pop music didn't feature. There was no record player. No transistors. Our huge, antique wireless set was tuned to the BBC Welsh Home Service. The only music I heard all week long came on Sunday afternoons, when *Caniadaeth y Cysegr* aired – congregational hymn-singing in Welsh. So I was teased mercilessly when I went out to play in the back lane, or up the *gwli* towards Hughes Street, by all the other kids, who thought it was hilarious that the only pop group I'd heard of was The Beatles. And that was only because the Fab Four were so thoroughly disapproved of in our house.

Up the Rhondda!

Yes, my education in music came late. But it couldn't have happened in a better place: Tonypandy Square. The Record Shop, opposite the Picturedrome, was a cavern of delights in the 1970s. Laid out in alphabetical order on rack after rack, just waiting for us to flip through them, were the sounds of the Seventies – the whole world of rock, soul, blues, jazz, even some classical music. Walking up Dunraven Street to Pandy Square from Penygraig, I had to pass Woolworth's and it was always tempting to pop in, especially when a special teenage friend of mine started her Saturday job on the tills there. But I would never have dreamt of buying a record in Woolies, even though it sold knock-off cover versions of all the hits for next to nothing. That would have been a betrayal of Mal Rees, proud owner of The Record Shop.

Mal, a local JP and a big figure in the Tonypandy Chamber of Trade, was a genial, if shrewd, presence behind the counter in his own emporium. Mal's wife Jean also appeared on occasion. She was the sister of two genuine Rhondda legends, actors Donald and Glyn Houston. Years later, as I've explained, I made a film with Glyn – he had a small part, but such presence on the screen that he stole the show. I always thought that something of her brothers' stardust rubbed off on Jean. But Mal – he wasn't exactly glamorous. He made no attempt to get 'down with the kids', dressing more like a solicitor or a schoolteacher. Yes, a teacher – and like the best teachers, he became more of a mentor and a guide than an instructor. We all became his pupils, us spotty adolescents, learning to be ourselves, flicking through album after album in those stacked racks, hesitating and changing our minds – and then hesitating all over again, before finally coughing up out of our precious savings *two pounds and thirty pence* (was it that much?) for a spanking new addition to our collection.

And that first record I bought? It wasn't heavy rock, or prog rock, or Bowie or Dylan or The Stones or anything particularly right-on: just fairly middle-of-the-road folk-influenced pop from the north of England. But I'm not ashamed of it. And it certainly made the cut when it came to deciding which of my records would move with us to our new house. It was Lindisfarne's *Fog on the Tyne*.

Us Record Shop regulars browsed much more than we bought. Most of us could only afford one purchase a month, but we spent hours there every Saturday morning all the same: discussing the current charts and the classic albums of years gone by, arguing about the latest releases and perhaps – like me, dreamer that I was – imagining we could become part of that whole scene ourselves, writing a great rock song, *The* Great Rhondda Rock Song. (My best effort was called *Tonypandy Ton-Up*: a bluesy beat, and lyrics with an authentic local setting and a touch of *cynghanedd* – that resonant consonantal chime of Welsh bardic tradition – colliding playfully with the thrills of speed and the open road. A sure-fire hit! If only…)

We talked about things other than music too – gossip and news and the way of the world. Mal magicked an atmosphere that never made us feel pressurised. He never seemed to mind however long we took, never failed to smile and give us a cheery "See you next week!", even if we eventually made our way back out onto Pandy Square without buying a single thing, not even a single. As a businessman, I'm sure The Record Shop gave him a decent living, but I sensed even then that that wasn't why he was doing it. He had an ear for music, and – well-advised by the series of 'Saturday boys' who served behind the counter, no doubt – he certainly was knowledgeable about his stock, keeping it up-to-the-minute and relevant, week after week, year after year, through all the fads and trends, false starts and naffnesses of 1970s pop and rock. But the real value that Mal provided was in something we could never have bought, no matter how long we teenagers saved up. His Record Shop was a shared space, and a safe one, where – however smart or slow we were, however cocky or insecure – we got an *education*. An education as much – probably more – from each other, as directly from Mal himself. An education in something that really mattered. Music. And it mattered not because it could help us pass an exam or get a job, but because it could be enjoyed for itself, appreciated for itself. Because (though we would hardly have said it like this) it was a thing of beauty.

I've been reading a book that was published recently – *The Sound of Being Human*, by the brilliant music journalist Jude Rogers. She's 20 years younger than me, but as I read about her Welsh upbringing and the wonderful range of artists she's loved at various stages of her life, her path seems to keep crossing my own musical journey. She writes about records and tapes and radio DJs and dancing, and she focuses her memories on 12 particular tracks, but her book is about much more than that. It's about how we rely on music for comfort, for insight, for connection with other people; how we grow with songs and how songs grow inside us. Music, says Jude Rogers, defines us as human beings. And do you know what? I'm certain Mal Rees would agree.

38
We Beat the All Blacks!

THE ALL BLACKS are coming! Every autumn nowadays, it seems, Wales renews a rugby rivalry that spans more than a century, and the entire planet. A rivalry that used to be a contest of equals. Now, as far as I know, New Zealand has never sent a team to play in the Rhondda – unlike the Australians, whose national team faced the might of Penygraig in 1908, if you remember. But despite Wales's dismal run of defeats, there *are* some Rhondda players who could respond to that famous rugby chant "Who beat the All Blacks?" with a resounding "We did!"

For the rugby fan, there's no disputing the fact that the All Blacks have a special aura. Against Wales, for far too long now, it's been an aura of invincibility. It's said whilst other teams remember their victories, New Zealand remember their defeats, and perhaps that's why there are so few of them. Sometimes there's been a dark edge to their play – a determination to win at any cost that seems counter to the spirit of the game. But when they're at their best, it takes something special to beat them. Their excellence encourages their opponents to rise the occasion. I don't know about you, but away from sport, I've met a handful of people who are a bit like that – people of real backbone, people who stick to their principles even if it's not in their narrow self-interest. They challenge you to bring out the best in yourself, not to beat them, but to live like them, to join them in living wholeheartedly for the best.

Anyway, back to the rugby: I *have* been fortunate enough to be there in person to see the All Blacks beaten, and it *did* take something special. In January 1973, the Barbarians famously won in Cardiff. Gareth Edwards scored *that* try. But it was Tylorstown's John Bevan whose determination took him over the line for the crucial score that took the game beyond New Zealand's grasp. John Bevan! The big wing already knew what it took to beat the men in black – he'd played for the Lions in New Zealand in 1971. And he'd sprinted 40 yards to power over for a try for Wales against the All Blacks, the month before that magical Barbarians game.

But he wasn't the only Rhondda man involved that day. There were two others who had crucial roles in broadcasting the Barbarians' sorcery.

Commentator Cliff Morgan was, of course, a great player himself: 29 Welsh caps, and 4 for the British & Irish Lions. He came from Trebanog, so he was a special favourite in our family, because when my father and his sister were growing up on Top Trebanog Road, Cliff was a near neighbour of similar age. Auntie Marion always boasted about going with him to Sunday School and Band of Hope.

Cliff's commentary is worthy of the try itself. Brilliant. The story goes that he was only commentating that day because Bill McLaren had lost his voice. But a former BBC colleague of mine looked up the *Radio Times* billing for the programme the other day, and it lists as commentator... Cliff Morgan. The *Radio Times* went to press a full ten days ahead of transmission, so it must have been planned for Cliff to be at the mike all along. Anyway, it's fair to say that no one, not even the legendary McLaren, could have done it better.

The other Rhondda man who got a credit in the *Radio Times* that day was Dewi Griffiths from Ton Pentre. In later years, Dewi was best known as the presenter of the long-running radio series *A String of Pearls*. Back in the 1970s, he was the BBC's top rugby director, responsible for the coverage of all of Wales's home games in that Golden Era. Indeed, I think it's fair to say that he helped to invent the way rugby was covered on television.

It's something viewers take for granted now, but it was a visual grammar that had to be developed – how to frame a shot of the scrum, for instance, to show the detail of the action without losing the broader picture of how play might develop. Nowadays, a battery of cameras covers every major international, and television match officials review play from every conceivable angle. In 1973, Dewi Griffiths had just four cameras to work with at the National Stadium: a wide-angle and a closer lens up in the South Stand; a third right beside the action down on the touchline; and a fourth behind the posts on the West Terrace. Dewi himself would have been in the shadow of the stands just yards away, sitting in the 'Scanner' – a big van kitted out as a mobile control room – pushing the buttons that cut the TV picture from one camera to another, and barking out a constant stream of instructions to all four camera operators. And Cliff Morgan would have had all that in his earpiece. Watch the try online carefully, and you'll see the four cameras used to capture all the drama of the play, and the crowd's reaction. It's a beautiful piece of direction precisely because normally you just don't notice it. The pictures are just right. Married to Cliff's commentary, it'll be watched for as long as sport endures.

Cliff Morgan also knew the thrill of beating the All Blacks as a player. In 1953, the Trebanog man played outside half for the Cardiff club side that defeated New Zealand 8-3. His performance that day merited not just praise in the sports pages of the *Western Mail*, but a whole editorial column, a space normally reserved for matters of deep political significance:

> We do not think that the passing of the years will ever dim for us the gleam and glory of the historic encounter at the

Cardiff Arms Park on Saturday, or tarnish the memory of Cliff Morgan's darting and swooping across the turf and skimming past every obstacle like a swift at play.

Cliff Morgan's half-back partner for Cardiff that day was Ystrad Rhondda-born Rex Willis, later the owner of a chain of cinemas across south Wales, including 'my' Plaza in Tonypandy. Outside them, on the wing, was Penygraig's Gareth Griffiths, the eldest of four brothers who all played for Cardiff. Gareth had won schoolboy caps for Wales when he was at Porth County. He, Rex Willis and Cliff Morgan were all picked for the international fixture against New Zealand later on that 1953 tour.

Cliff at No. 10. It was a kind of tradition. Another Rhondda Cliff – Cliff Jones, born in Porth – had played outside half for Wales against the All Blacks in 1935. Back then, the Rhondda man was a controversial choice: his inclusion split the Swansea half-back unit of Haydn Tanner and Willie Davies, the precocious teenage cousins who'd been key to Swansea's victory over the All Blacks three months before. As it turned out, Cliff Jones's selection for the national side was vindicated, even though the margin of Wales's victory couldn't have been tighter: a single point, 13-12.

Back to 1953. The three Rhondda Cardiffians – Cliff Morgan, Rex Willis, Gareth Griffiths – were joined in the full Welsh side by Penygraig hooker Dai Davies. In the second half of the match, Gareth Griffiths dislocated his shoulder and had to leave the field. No substitutes were allowed in those days, even for injuries. So Gareth simply lay down on a blanket on the touchline, grimaced whilst the shoulder was put back in place by the WRU doctor, and then joined the fray again. A Penygraig hero, right enough! Wales triumphed 13 points to 8, and so the Rhondda quartet were all part of that last Wales team who can say "We beat the All Blacks!"

We Beat the All Blacks was the title we gave to a TV documentary I was involved in making, about the famous

Llanelli victory in 1972. The players in that match had some great stories to tell on camera – about what happened before, during and *after* the game on the day when, in a town that boasted several breweries, the delirious supporters drank the pubs dry. In another programme I oversaw, Eddie Butler went out to New Zealand to tell the story of how John Bevan and the 1971 Lions beat the All Blacks in their own backyard.

But there was one much older victory over New Zealand which I was determined to make a programme about – and that was a *real* challenge. After all, there was no archive footage of the game played in Cardiff in 1905, and everyone involved was long dead. But when the centenary of the match approached, I had personal reasons to make sure it was marked properly on screen. Although there was no film to be had, the occasion was vivid in my mind's eye: my grandfather, Tommy John, was one of the 47,000 people who crowded into Cardiff Arms Park on that December afternoon and saw Wales win – the only time on that 35-match tour that the All Blacks were defeated. Grampa never tired of telling us about what he witnessed that day, and when he died, nearly 70 years afterwards, it was one of the facts of his life the *Rhondda Leader* highlighted in his obituary: *he was there!*

So in memory of Tommy John, as much as of the match itself, I set about getting a commission to make a TV film to celebrate the centenary. My idea – since there was no footage and no living witnesses – was to reconstruct the match using the detailed, play-by-play newspaper accounts published at the time. We had two full teams in period costume, who were drilled in how to replay the game's key moves in exact detail. And using what was then state-of-the-art computer graphics, we morphed thirty well-togged-out 'extras' into a crowd of 47,000, filling our 'virtual' Arms Park. It looked terrific – and it sounded great too, because that was the first time the crowd took up the singing of our national anthem in response to the New Zealand *haka*. As our camera panned over the crowd

191

we'd dressed in Edwardian finery, the man who first picks up the cue to sing '*Hen Wlad Fy Nhadau*' along with the team is – in my mind anyway – none other than my grandfather, Tommy John.

Tommy John wasn't the only Penygraig man there that day. On the field of play – at wing three-quarter – was a near neighbour of his. He's listed in the official match programme along with the club he played for: *Willie Llewellyn (Penygraig)*. And in a game between the era's two outstanding sides, which had been billed as a world championship decider, it was a dazzling pre-planned move featuring the three-quarters which won the game for Wales. New Zealand always claimed they'd scored an equalising try of their own; but with a mountain of forensic evidence culled from those newspaper reports, our film came to the firm conclusion that the referee was perfectly correct to disallow their score. And the jury of the Celtic Film Festival, no less, agreed with our verdict – they awarded us their top prize, the Gold Torc for Spirit of the Festival. So we must have been right!

Willie Llewellyn was probably the first Rhondda man who could say he beat the All Blacks. And there was a strange upshot to his part in that famous victory. Five years later, during the industrial dispute that's become known as the Tonypandy Riots, there was widespread damage to the retail premises of Dunraven Street. Every shop, it was said, had its windows smashed in by the vast crowd of miners who'd been locked out of their places of work. Every shop, bar one – the chemist's owned and run by a Mr Willie Llewellyn of Penygraig.

39

Tonypandy Riots!

'IT'S THAT TIME of year again', as the Stereophonics put it. Early November. We've put the clocks back. But imagine if we were to put them back much, much further. Imagine... it's early November *1910*.

12,000 Mid-Rhondda miners are on strike. From Porth to Ystrad, every colliery is at a standstill. Negotiations with the coal owners have broken down. There's no knowing when or if they'll resume. And then something happens that turns this industrial dispute into something else again, something almost mythical. Not just a battle for who controls the conditions under which the miners labour, hundreds of feet below the Rhondda, to dig up the Black Diamond – and the power and wealth it represents. No, this is also a battle for the kind of place that, above ground, the Rhondda will become, the kind of lives that Rhondda people will lead, the kind of social order they will show is possible.

It's a clash of massive forces. On one side, the Chief Constable of Glamorgan, the Metropolitan Police, the Lancashire Fusiliers, the 18th Hussars and Winston Churchill. On the other, those 12,000 Mid-Rhondda miners and their families. It's going to be a Riot...

To mark the centenary of those events, I produced and directed a BBC documentary: *Tonypandy Riots*. It made the news. The film looked back from 2010 through the eyes of four local people – singing star Sophie Evans; Penygraig rugby player Derwyn Nicholas; Tonypandy College community manager Julie Atkins; and ambulance controller David Gwilym Jones. We had expert help from other Rhondda people – historian David Maddox, miner Ivor England and the Chief Constable of South Wales, Peter Vaughan. The whole programme was built on the foundations of a lifetime's academic research and thinking about what happened in 1910 by another son of the Rhondda, Professor Dai Smith, a friend and colleague of mine for many years.

We thought of our project as 'A New History'. We closed the streets of Tonypandy for a few hours so that hundreds of twenty-first-century schoolchildren could be filmed marching in the footsteps of their great-grandparents, and holding their own mass meeting in the middle of Dunraven Street to pay tribute to them, exactly a century later. It was advance notice of the plan to do that which caught the eyes of the newshounds. One of them phoned me to say that he'd be coming along with a camera crew of his own. "I understand you're going to shut off the shopping centre so that you can re-stage the Tonypandy Riots," he said. Not quite. We'd worked carefully with the schools to ensure that the behaviour and the tone adopted by the youngsters was strong and challenging, but properly respectful of public order and the presence of a handful of constabulary members, who were there – one hundred years on – to help, not to hinder.

"We gather here today," proclaimed the generation of 2010 when they reached the town centre, their amplified words echoing up and down the street and captured on camera for posterity, "to remember the Rhondda's coal industry on the centenary of the Cambrian Combine Dispute of 1910. We think of all those who were affected by that dispute and of everyone associated with our long and proud history of mining. We are mindful that the true price of coal was the sacrifice made and the hardship endured by the miners and their families, so that others could enjoy warmth and power. We are grateful for their vision and determination that the riches of the world we live in should be shared fairly by all of us."

Our finished documentary was designed to remind them and the watching viewers of the truth of what had occurred right there on Dunraven Street a hundred years before. But why? Why does what happened so long ago matter? Why has it resounded down the long decades since? And what does it mean for us now? Big questions, important questions for what the Rhondda has been, for what it is; indeed, for what Wales could be, will be. It took me three long episodes of *John on the Rhondda* to try to answer them.

The Dunraven Street of 1910 was a retail paradise built to trade on the wealth that Rhondda coal had generated: milliners, drapers, flannel merchants, outfitters, ironmongers, shoe and boot shops, all the latest fashions. Edwardian Tonypandy boasts a whole class of shopkeepers – they're big players on the local scene. One of them, as we've just heard, is more than that. Willie Llewellyn the chemist was on the wing for Wales in the legendary win over the 1905 All Blacks. He's a hero to everyone in Mid-Rhondda. But not all the shopkeepers are loved. Some of them own terraced houses where the miners and their families live – and they lease them on condition that the miners spend their wages in (you've guessed it) the very shops they own.

Ah, those wages. How they're calculated is crucial to what happens. The miners don't get an hourly rate, a weekly wage or a monthly salary. They're paid according to the weight of sellable coal they can cut. Getting the coal isn't easy (to repeat a cliché, if it was, anyone could do it). It sits in thin seams, sandwiched between hard, useless rock, laid down millions of years ago. Digging it out takes huge physical effort. And once the most accessible coal is won, the miners have to go to places where the bands of rock have faults, where there's stone mixed in with the coal, where the groundwater floods in. The crunch comes at the Ely Pit in Penygraig, over the price per ton that's going to be paid for work on a new seam – the Upper Five Foot. Everybody knows it's going to cause problems.

But this isn't just about pounds, shillings and pence. It's about a young generation of miners' leaders, about their vision of a better way to run their industry – indeed their whole world. They're impatient with the old-style miners' agent, William Abraham – 'Mabon', to give him the bardic name he liked to use. Mabon believes in co-operating with the mine-owners. But there's a new breed of mine-owner – tough, modern, business-minded. Step forward D A Thomas, shortly to be made Baron Rhondda. Thomas merges Mid-Rhondda's pits into a single company, the Cambrian Combine. He's determined to flex its industrial muscle to drive down costs. In other words, lower wages.

Across the summer of 1910, deadlock: the miners in the Ely Pit won't accept the new rates. So on 1 September, D A Thomas shuts the colliery gates against them, putting them out of work. It's a lockout. Miners in the other Mid-Rhondda pits come out in solidarity, but Mabon scolds them back to work: they've no legal basis for striking without notice. So the union lodges serve that notice – a strike will begin on 1 November. Mabon – as ever – seeks to negotiate, boasting that he's close enough to the mine owner to get him to cough up a few pennies more, and that he knows him well enough to bring some leverage to bear: "My friend D. A. Thomas has been suffering from poor health; and I feel sure that on his holiday in France he will not benefit… if he were to hear of a strike such as this."

Mabon's attempt at compromise is resoundingly rejected by the men. And now the owners dig in. They refuse point blank to talk further. So on 1 November, all of Mid-Rhondda's miners come out on strike. D A Thomas isn't worried: it turns out that he's made a deal with the other coal-owners across south Wales. They'll indemnify the Cambrian Combine against its operating losses, however long the strike goes on. Thomas can sit and wait until the starving miners have had enough. When word gets back to the Strike Committee, they realise that their only chance of winning is to hit the Cambrian Combine hard and fast where it hurts – in its assets. If maintenance work can be stopped, D A Thomas's pits will be at risk of permanent damage by flood and rockfall, forcing him back to the negotiating table.

So on 7 November, summoned by bugle and marching behind the Tonypandy Fife Band, miners and their families – thousands of them – tramp from pithead to pithead, stopping the machinery that keeps the collieries ticking over. Fires are raked out, boilers and ventilating fans shut down, electric generators silenced. There's little opposition until they arrive at what we used to call the Scotch Colliery, on Llwynypia Road, Tonypandy. Here stands the citadel the owners have chosen to defend, a symbol of their property-owning rights: the colliery's Engine House, the Power House. It's literally a power struggle.

The police are here. The Chief Constable, Lionel Lindsay, a good friend of the coal-owners, has mustered every officer he can find. Underground: three hundred pit ponies, deliberately left down there by the owners, though there's been no work for them since the strike began. These mute hostages will drown, deep in the flooded roadways, if the electric pumps are shut down. But should the ponies perish, D A Thomas reckons that public opinion will turn against the miners.

At the colliery gates, the miners demand to speak to the maintenance crews inside, claiming their rights of peaceful picketing. The police refuse. The stand-off gets tense. At nine o'clock that evening, there's a change of shift inside the Power House. Youths try to rush the police guard at the gateway. Will John, the miners' leader, appeals for calm from what's now a huge crowd. But stones are thrown. The police charge. There's hand-to-hand fighting. The miners are driven back to

Tonypandy Square. There, well beyond midnight now, they continue to defy the police. The Chief Constable, terrified that he'll lose control completely, telegraphs for the troops to be sent in.

What happens next has been a matter of fierce debate ever since – in the House of Commons, in the minds of historians and in the cafés and pubs of Tonypandy. Did Home Secretary Winston Churchill send in the troops against unarmed British citizens who'd been locked out of their place of work?

What's not disputed is that on the morning after those disturbances at the Scotch Colliery, thousands of miners came together for a mass meeting at the Mid-Rhondda Athletic Ground to decide on their next move. A telegram is read out to them, a telegram from Churchill in London which seems to bear out what he and his family always claimed – that rather than sending in the troops, Churchill held them back:

> You may give the following message from me to the miners. Their best friends here are greatly distressed at the trouble which has broken out and will do their best to help them meet fair treatment... But rioting must cease at once so that the inquiry shall not be prejudiced and to prevent the credit of the Rhondda Valley being injured. Confiding in the good sense of the Cambrian Combine workmen, we are holding back the soldiers for the present and sending police instead. Winston Churchill.

There was a precedent for sending armed troops to confront striking miners, a shameful one: the 'Featherstone Massacre' of 1893. It ended with soldiers shooting Yorkshire miners dead. Churchill seems desperate to avoid any repeat. And satisfied that armed forces *aren't* going to be deployed against them, the Tonypandy miners leave the Mid-Rhondda Ground to march down to the Power House to resume their peaceful picket. But that's not how it turns out.

The police refuse to let them speak to the blackleg workers who are keeping the pumps operating, preventing the Scotch Colliery from being flooded and D A Thomas from suffering damage to one of his key assets. At five o'clock, the stone-throwing starts. The Power House windows that face the roadway are shattered. The Chief Constable gives the order for mounted police to clear the road. They charge forward. The battle lasts for two hours. Wooden palings are ripped down for weapons. There are baton charges. The police make good use of their truncheons. Hundreds of men are injured, many with head wounds. Later, one miner, Samuel Rays (or possibly Rhys), dies from skull injuries.

A panicked local magistrate sends again for troops: "Police cannot cope with rioters at Llwynypia. Troops... absolutely necessary for further protection." And this time, less than 24 hours after the promise he's telegrammed to the miners, Churchill acquiesces in the request. He messages the military commander, Major General Nevil Macready: "As the situation appears to have become more serious you should, if the Chief Constable or Local Authority desire it, move all the cavalry into the district without delay."

Pushed back now to Tonypandy Square, the battered miners regroup. In front of them, the mayhem at the Power House. Behind them, Dunraven Street, the retail paradise that's been built for them. That's where they turn. Windows are smashed, shops ransacked, goods stolen. The damage is estimated in the tens of thousands of pounds – probably millions at today's values. In the press, it's dubbed *'Tonypandemonium'*.

But this isn't a mob without a mind. As Dai Smith has said, "The crowd is not organised, but it knows what to do." One of the few shops left undamaged was that chemist's owned by local rugby hero Willie Llewellyn: his exploits in helping Wales beat the All Blacks aren't forgotten, even in the heat of riot.

Riot? You could call it that, certainly. But looked at another way, it's a Rising: a brief but deliberate act of defiance by downtrodden people. A Rising against their masters, the coal-owners who would deny them a living wage; a Rising against the class of shopkeepers, who – with exceptions – want to define the Rhondda their way, as a community they can profit from, preside over and control; a Rising against the state which, despite the assurances of the Home Secretary, seems willing to use all its might on one side of the argument.

At lunchtime the next day, the troops arrive – the 18th Hussars, wearing khaki service dress and carrying carbine swords, and the Lancashire Fusiliers, who take their rifles and bayonets to their billets in Llwynypia. Because they're not here on a day trip. There will be troops in Tonypandy well into the following year.

But their commander General Macready is less willing to go along with the demands of the coal-owners and the panicking local magistrates than they may have anticipated. His calm assessment of the stand-off at the Power House confirms what historians say – that the miners were never trying to occupy the colliery, they were responding to what they saw as the owners and police colluding to make a symbolic stand against them:

> Investigations on the spot convinced me that the original reports regarding the attacks on the mines on November 8th had been exaggerated. What were described as 'desperate attempts' to sack the power-house at Llwynypia proved to have been an attempt to force the gateway, against which an ample force of police under the Chief Constable was available on the spot… had the mob been as numerous or so determined as the reports implied, there was nothing to have prevented them from overrunning the whole premises. That they did not was due less to the action of the police than to

the want of leading or inclination to proceed to extremities on the part of the strikers.

All the same, Macready's troops are effectively an army of occupation. They ensure that mass demonstrations against blackleg labour will be ineffective. They nullify the picketing which the leaders of the strike had seen as their only hope of victory. And they do come into direct contact with the strikers. Bayonets are used for what's described as 'a little gentle persuasion'. The miners and their families can do little but eke out their meagre strike pay and stand firm together.

The troops are out in massive force in December, when 13 miners are summoned to Pontypridd Magistrates Court to stand trial for their part in the 'Riots'. Bugle calls echo through Mid-Rhondda once again. Accompanied by drum and fife bands, 10,000 people answer the call, marching down to Ponty to support those the authorities are determined to make an example of. It's a remarkable demonstration of solidarity. At the head of the mile-long procession, a banner proclaims the defiance of the miners – 'Hungry as L', it seems to say, the 'L' written as an oversized capital letter. But viewed closer up, it actually reads 'Hungry as Lions'.

Food *is* an issue, though. As winter draws on, the children of Tonypandy are being fed in soup kitchens. A London newspaper reporter writes that the brooding, sullen atmosphere up and down the streets of the Rhondda is like something he's experienced in Russia, in those years leading up to the overthrow of the Tsar. There's revolution in the air. Outgunned, the miners are losing the battle – but who will win the war?

Now that the troops are here, the miners can't stop D A Thomas using blacklegs to keep his pits ticking over. He can wait and wait and wait, indemnified against his losses by other coal-owners, until the toll on the miners' families becomes too much to bear. It takes ten long months, but eventually, hungry and still angry, the men are forced back to work. All their efforts seem in vain. Those going back to toil in the Ely Pit's difficult Upper Five Foot Seam won't earn a ha'penny more for each ton of sellable coal they cut than D A Thomas offered before the strike began, in the compromise brokered back then by William Abraham, 'Mabon'. A million pounds has been lost in wages. And for a quarter of the Mid-Rhondda workforce, 3,000 men, the outcome is even worse: the owners say their labour isn't needed any longer.

It's a bitter defeat. But 'Tonypandy' sparks a national debate. The iniquity of denying colliers a fair wage when they are struggling to dig out enough coal to keep their families fed, from seams that are fractured and full of stone, triggers widespread demands for an earnings safety net. A year after the Mid-Rhondda miners return to work, the government brings in a Minimum Wage Act. It may be the most valuable legacy of the Tonypandy Riots – a principle as relevant and as debated today as was back in 1912.

Something else happens that year, something that shows that all of this has been about more than wage-rates. In Mid-Rhondda, the new generation of union leaders publish *The Miners' Next Step*. It's only the miners themselves, they argue, who have the real, 'hands-on' expertise in how to work a coalmine. Unless they're in charge of their own working lives, the industry's problems will never be solved. But the answer they put forward in this visionary manifesto isn't nationalisation – state ownership. In any dispute, *that* would just bring colliers into conflict with the forces of the state. And Tonypandy knows from painful experience what that means. *The Miners' Next Step* wants mines controlled by the miners themselves: not by the coal-owners, not by the government, not even by full-time union officials like Mabon. All leaders become corrupt, it declares, however noble their intentions. "No man was ever good enough, or strong enough, to have such power at his disposal, as real leadership implies."

It's a breathtaking set of proposals. It could only have come from a working class who'd lived through the Cambrian Combine Dispute. More than half a century later, when the *nationalised* coal industry was convulsed by the disputes of the 1970s and 1980s, its warning about the forces of the state being used against the miners took on a prophetic tone.

And what of Churchill? His name was never revered in south Wales like it was elsewhere. In Rhondda cinemas, his appearances in newsreels were booed. His defeat in the General Election after the war was cheered loudly – and paved the way for the creation of the welfare state and the NHS. 40 years after the events of 1910, 'Tonypandy' still irks Churchill so much that he uses a speech in Cardiff to preach what he calls 'the true story'. He stopped the movement of troops, he claims, and sent in the Metropolitan Police with the sole object of preventing loss of life. Well, maybe... up to a point. He did stop the troops. For just one day. But then they *did* come, they *did* stay, and they *were* used. In fact, they were key to the outcome of the strike. So, when Churchill says the troops were kept in the background, that all contact with the miners was by London police armed with nothing but rolled-up mackintoshes, he's doing more than being economical with the truth. He's *lying* to protect his own reputation.

So who did 'win' the Cambrian Combine Dispute? Churchill? The Metropolitan Police and the British Army? The Chief Constable of Glamorgan? D A Thomas? *He* might have been ennobled as Baron Rhondda, but in the long run it *wasn't* coal magnates like him who got to define what the Rhondda was, what the Rhondda is, at its best, when it lives up to its true values. And it *wasn't* the shopkeepers of Tonypandy – as noble as *some* of them were – who got to decide what kind of community they could do business in. Rhondda's social ambitions weren't limited even by Mabon, with his beguiling notions of compromise, that 'half a loaf was better than no loaf at all'.

No, it was the miners themselves and their families who used the lessons of 1910 to redefine the Rhondda. And what a glorious, far-sighted vision it was. To them, the Rhondda was a community built on solidarity: on being solid with each other, on looking out for each other in tough times, on what my father used to call 'stickability' – sticking it out and sticking together. In my book, that's true nobility.

You might say I'm being starry-eyed about this – about what the Rhondda was, and is. Fair enough. We all know of times when Rhondda people haven't lived up to those ideals. But I bet we can think of occasions when we *have* – when we've stood up for each other, and with each other, in really important ways. The courage and sacrifice of NHS staff, carers, teachers, bus drivers, binmen and many others in the pandemic is just one example. In every part of the Rhondda, you'll find small stories that shout one big message – this is a place where people put people before profit, where what matters to 'us' matters more than what matters to 'me'.

The pits are gone now, the events of 1910 passed out of living memory. Mid-Rhondda is a changed place. Where the Ely miners went to work, children take their lessons in Nantgwyn School. The Scotch Colliery pithead, to quote Max Boyce, is a supermarket now. And time has done to the Power House, the mine-owners' citadel, what the strikers couldn't, or rather, never intended, to do. But – to echo the words spoken by those schoolchildren in my BBC documentary, those marching schoolchildren who are progenies of Tonypandy's radicalism – in their vision that the riches of the world we live in should be shared fairly, and in their determination to face up to forces that seemed much more powerful than they were, the miners of Mid-Rhondda proclaimed that the labour of working people should never again be taken for granted, and showed that they were capable of imagining a world that works in the interests of us all.

40
Penrhys

YOU MAY THINK you know all about Penrhys. It's a place that's weathered storms and emerged as something of a model community, a skyline village way above the Rhondda.

It *is* high up. There's a joke we used to crack when I was a boy: *Why is Penrhys the highest mountain in the world? Because it's above The Star!* I know, it's the way I tell them, isn't it? But Penrhys has another claim to fame – one that doesn't depend on the name of the old pub at the bottom of the hill, one that goes back hundreds and hundreds of years. I wonder if you know the full story? It's a bit of a thriller...

In 2012, I produced and directed *The Story of Wales*, a 'landmark' BBC series which covered the whole history of our nation, from 30,000 years ago to the present day. We did a fair amount of filming in the Rhondda – how could we ignore our central role in the crowning of King Coal, the industry that shaped and defined modern Wales? But there was a much older tale set in the valley which I was also determined to tell. And, drawing on the expertise of historian Professor Madeleine Gray, that's what we did.

We focused on an incident that happened on Penrhys when Henry VIII was on the throne. Back then, the whole population of Wales would have been smaller than modern-day Cardiff's. Cardiff scarcely existed. There *were* some towns – Carmarthen, Haverfordwest, Brecon, Wrexham. But the vast majority of people were farming in places like the Rhondda, living in – and off – the countryside. Nine out of every ten of them didn't speak or understand any English. Most of them never had the luxury of travelling far from their own parish. Their lives were lived in a tight locality – *y filltir sgwar*, their own patch – something that's still so important in many parts of Wales.

Families were large, but disease and food shortages meant many children never lived to be adults. In the teeth of hardship and tragedy, people held fast to traditional beliefs. The Welsh were devout Catholics, known across Europe for their devotion to the Virgin Mary. Their Christianity sat alongside the faith they had in more ancient rites and rituals, like the healing powers of holy wells and springs.

But a big change was coming, driven by Henry VIII's ambitions – and his sex life. Henry's desire to annul his marriage to Catherine of Aragon, his brother's widow, sparked a break with the Pope in Rome. Henry used the split to get his hands not just on a new wife, but also on money and property – and lots of it. He seized the wealth of the monasteries, which for centuries had been pillars of Welsh life, chronicling our history, counselling our princes, sponsoring our poets. Henry's avarice suited those Protestants who were determined to smash Catholic practices in Wales, and they targeted six key sites sacred to the Old Faith. One of these was Penrhys. But Henry's enforcer, Thomas Cromwell, knew that they needed to move very carefully. This was one of the holiest places in Wales.

For centuries, pilgrims had been coming to Penrhys 'across land and sea', according to the poets. They came to bathe in the waters of the holy well, expecting to be healed or blessed. The Cistercian monks of Llantarnam in Gwent had an outlying sheep farm or grange on Penrhys, and by the fifteenth century there were three large buildings here: the well, a chapel, and a hostelry – the first pub in the Rhondda, I suppose. It offered accommodation for pilgrims. And their numbers were dramatically on the up, because Penrhys was home to a wooden statue which had appeared in an oak tree here as if by a miracle: a statue of the Virgin Mary bending to kiss the baby Jesus, who she's holding in her arms. She's the Queen of Heaven. But she's also an ordinary peasant woman, giving her child a *cwtsh*. I'm sure that's what spoke to the ordinary folk of the valley: she was one of theirs, a woman of the Rhondda.

By Henry VIII's time, the pilgrimage to Penrhys had become hugely popular. Miracles were said to happen here. It's easy to look back now and write that off as superstition, Professor Gray reminded us. Back then, she stressed, it was a conviction that ran right through society, from kings and queens down to the poorest peasant: the belief that, if you make the effort to travel to somewhere where holy things have happened, good things can happen to you.

But for the Protestant reformers who'd been empowered by Henry, beliefs like these were not just superstitious: they endangered national security. With the threat of Spain in the offing, Catholics were viewed – potentially, at least – as traitors. For Thomas Cromwell, it was a political priority to destroy shrines like Penrhys, to break the hold they had on people's faith. No matter how beautiful they were, no matter how much they were loved – in fact, precisely because they were beautiful, and people loved them.

So in the summer of 1538, Cromwell writes to William Herbert, the son of the Sheriff of Monmouthshire, of St Julian's in Newport, and orders him to ride to Penrhys. He's given a mission: to destroy the shrine. When he arrives, there's a stand-off. Local people gather, reluctant to let this outsider snatch the statue they venerate. Herbert needs to impress on them all the authority he's been given by the Crown. What he says in his report to Thomas Cromwell is along the lines of, "I explained to them what they were doing wrong, how they were dishonouring the King and God. And I took the statue away." End of story!

Well, not quite. The strange thing is that it takes William Herbert three weeks to write his report. And when he does, he has to admit that the statue is still in his house in Newport. *Why on earth is it still there?* That statue is hot! It could spark a rebellion. What's he doing with it in his house?

Was William Herbert a secret Catholic sympathiser? In an era when Catholics' loyalties were highly suspect, he *did* arrange to marry his son into one of the foremost Catholic families of Monmouthshire. But if Herbert was having second thoughts about Penrhys's miraculous statue, the reality is that Cromwell was far too powerful a man to be denied. The wooden statue *was* eventually sent to London. At Tyburn – the place where traitors were executed – the statue was burnt to cinders. The shrine was destroyed and the pilgrimage stopped. The well, of course, didn't dry up. People kept using it. They said it was good for helping their butter to churn.

Traditions about the spring endure to the present day. "You can go to Penrhys and find there's hardly any water," says Madeleine Gray. "You can go there and find plenty. The locals say it flows when it wants to. So there is still *something* about the place, despite Thomas Cromwell's determination to erase every trace of its magic."

The beautiful stone statue of the Virgin and her Christ-child which stands on the ridge up above the well nowadays is proof that Cromwell didn't completely succeed. For Catholics, Penrhys's miraculous associations with Mary put it technically on a par with shrines like Lourdes and Fátima, places that attract millions of pilgrims from all over the world. So Penrhys has constantly been recognised and revered. And in recent years, its national significance has been reasserted, with the opening of the Penrhys Pilgrimage Way as a recognised hiking route, bringing the faithful (and those who simply enjoy a good walk!) all the way from Llandaff Cathedral in Cardiff.

To me – born, like thousands of other Rhondda people, in a hospital on the mountainside just below the little chapel and the spring – Penrhys has always been somewhere that's precious, if not holy. I'm drawn back there again and again: just to gaze down on my birthplace, to lift up my eyes to the hills beyond Treorchy, to let my sight linger on Mid-Rhondda and all that it means to me. People have been coming here for centuries, thoughtfully, reverently, to ponder the deep mysteries of life, in the hope of better things to come. And that, for me, irrespective of anything else that might be true about the place, makes Penrhys very special indeed.

41

The Man Who Made Tommy Farr

I GOT MY hair cut this morning. Well, I say *'cut'*... what really happened is that the fuzz on top of my head was shaved. It's been a good few years now since I gave up the fight with male pattern baldness. I've gone for the shaven-headed look. Even my best friends call it 'brutal'.

All the same, the *notion* that my hair was being cut was enough to bring back a sliver of memory from early childhood – just some hazy images really, but something that connects me, however loosely, to one of the Great Rhondda Stories, an event that sent the name of Tonypandy resounding around the world.

I've only ever been really happy with my hairstyle in one short period of my life: my early twenties. It was 1978, or early '79. My hair was shoulder-length, dark with some auburn tints, and complemented by a full, bushy beard and moustache. When I washed and combed it properly, you might have mistaken me for a member of the Eagles. When it *wasn't* all washed and combed, I probably looked more like a caveman. It was a reaction, I suppose, to all those boyhood 'short back and sides' that Mam made me have, packing me off to Toni's, down at the bottom of Tylacelyn hill, by Jones the Fruiterer's. He might have been Italian, Toni, but Latin style and Roman culture seemed to have passed him by. In an era of Beatle cuts and mop tops, he left me and my cowlick stuck in the early 1950s, like some mini-GI who'd escaped from the Korean War.

But the recollection that came to me this morning was not the trauma of Toni's. It was from much earlier, when I wasn't old enough to go to the barber's by myself, and my Grampa, Tommy John, used to take me. Elwyn's was a proper old-fashioned barbershop up in Penygraig, in a little terrace adjoining the Labour Club, opposite Soar Chapel. It's all been demolished now, to make way for a roundabout.

In my memory, Elwyn looked like Harry Secombe and was just as jolly, but it's not really him or the haircut he gave me that's remained imprinted sharply on my mind. It's what happened afterwards, when I emerged short-haired onto the pavement outside, holding Tommy John's hand and blinking into the late afternoon sun.

"Look!" said Grampa, pointing across the road to the garage on the corner, where Penygraig Road turned up the hill. The garage had a couple of antiquated petrol pumps in front of it. Behind them, resting on a chair, or maybe just an upturned crate, savouring the last of the sunshine and looking like he owned the place – which I think he probably did – a walking stick propped up alongside him and a wry smile on his face, was a wrinkled old man. A man with one leg.

"Look," Grampa said again, "that's Joby Churchill!"

Joby Churchill, some say, was the man who made Tommy Farr. And Tommy Farr was the Tonypandy Terror, the tough, raw Rhondda boxer who seemed to be able to take any amount of punishment, and who took the legendary Joe Louis, the Brown Bomber, the full 15 rounds in an epic fight for the World Heavyweight Championship in Yankee Stadium, New York in 1937.

Tommy Farr had been born in 1913 in Clydach Vale, one of eight children. He started boxing at 12, went down the pit at 14, and retired from coal mining at the grand old age of 16, determined to make his living as a boxer. He'd already had scores of fights in the boxing booths of the day, and now he embarked on scores more: professional bouts, up and down the Valleys and further afield. He was brave and willing, but he was pretty naïve in the ring, *and* in the money matters and dark deals that surrounded the fight game. In those early days, he seemed to lose as often as he won. And his earnings were next to nothing.

There's a story about him having to walk home all the way from London, left penniless after one his many defeats. It was Joby Churchill he turned to then, and that was the shrewdest move he ever made. The one-legged saddler understood ringcraft, what it takes to win a fight; but, like all great coaches, what really counted was that he understood people. He lifted the young boxer's spirits and got him back on track. To Farr, he wasn't just a coach, a trainer and a mentor; he was a father figure, berating him, cajoling him, comforting him in just the right mixture to bring out the best in his talents, and the steel in his character.

Farr rarely knocked anyone out. But thanks to Joby Churchill, he added guile to courage, and learned how to wear his opponents down. There were still frustrations, but in a few short months in 1937, the stars all aligned for him. He became British and Empire Champion, before beating former world champ Max Baer on points. And then he *did* knock someone out – the German tank, Walter Neusel. And he did it in front of Hitler's Ambassador to Great Britain, Joachim von Ribbentrop. The British press went wild about Farr's victory: he'd beaten the Nazis! So, finally, Tommy Farr got his big break – a match with the great Joe Louis, for the Heavyweight Championship of the World.

It was Joby Churchill who went with the Tonypandy Terror, crossing the Atlantic with him in luxury on the *Queen Mary*, and standing in his corner at the packed-out Yankee Stadium, encouraging him between rounds with a few phrases in Welsh, as the fight went on… and on.

Back in Tonypandy, in the middle of the night, my Grampa and my father – not to mention everyone else in Wales, it seems – were glued to every word of the radio commentary, relayed 'live' for the first time down the transatlantic cable. Farr was a huge underdog: no one really gave him a chance of surviving more than a round or two. But he took Joe Louis the distance, sticking at it through 14 bruising rounds, and rallying strongly in the 15th and last, making his supporters believe he'd done enough to win.

It wasn't to be. But his battling efforts, his tenacity, and the craft that Joby Churchill had instilled in him won him friends and fans on both sides of the Atlantic. He was a celebrity now: big news, his name and that of his hometown on everyone's lips. Home he came, to Tonypandy, to a hero's welcome.

I have two other small connections to the Tommy Farr story. One Easter – I wasn't much older than the day I saw Joby Churchill – my parents took me and my grandparents on holiday to Bournemouth. We were in the Winter Gardens and it was getting dark. I was shouting excitedly to my Dad as we played ball on the grass. A couple walking their dog approached us. The man had recognised my Rhondda accent. He was living down there on the south coast of England – but he was Tommy Farr's brother. A long conversation with my grandfather, Tommy John, ensued: shared memories, people they both knew.

Bored, I suppose, I interrupted them to ask what the dog's name was. "Ask him," said the man, smiling. I was young, but old enough to know that a dog couldn't tell you its name. "No, really, what's his name?" "Ask him," I was told once more. Because, yes, you've guessed, the dog was called *Askim*. It was a piece of mischievous Rhondda wordplay transported to the seaside resorts of southern England, and though I'm sure Joby Churchill didn't have anything to do with it, in my childish imagination, the two things became connected

– the intelligence of the coach, and the wit expressed in a pet's moniker. Making a name for yourself, I decided, wasn't about hitting hard; it was about boxing clever. That's what turned the underdog into a top dog. It was what he'd learned from Joby Churchill which made all the difference for Tommy Farr, the difference between being just another journeyman boxer, and a hero whose sporting glory would be remembered a century later.

My final connection to Tommy Farr is pure coincidence. My grandfather died when I was 14. Right next to where he's buried in Trealaw Cemetery there's a much more impressive memorial. A carved white angel stands between four black marble pillars supporting a cut-stone roof topped by a cross. The Tonypandy Terror had that constructed for his parents, and he too now lies there. Tommy John and Tommy Farr, two heroes of mine, separated by a few feet of Rhondda clay. And just yards away from both of them, in direct line of sight – as I've only just discovered thanks to someone who had listened to me telling this story in my *John on the Rhondda* podcast – stands the headstone of another Rhondda titan, a titan with one leg: 'Job Churchill (Saddler), died November 7, 1963, aged 86 years. Always in our thoughts'.

42
Sunday School

IS YOUR FAMILY *Chapel* or *Pub*? It's not a question that means so much anymore, but when I was growing up in the Rhondda, it was the Great Divide. Whether it was the chapel or the pub which you frequented mattered like… well, I almost said 'hell', but you know what I mean. Chapel deacons frowned on any good Christian who entered licensed premises, and those who enjoyed the convivial atmosphere of a pub or club were rarely, if ever, seen in the pews of Bethania or Jerusalem, Soar or Saron. So it was Chapel *or* Pub. If you went to one, it was odds-on you never darkened the door of the other.

My family were Chapel. My Mam and Dad – lifelong teetotallers – were probably well into their fifties before they ever went into a pub, and then it was only if they were on their travels and there was nowhere else to get a square meal. But we're talking about the 1970s now, and pub lunches were just becoming a thing. Before then, you'd never have dreamt of entering into a Public House *for food*; and Mam and Dad certainly wouldn't countenance going there for a drink. No, when I was a boy, it was Chapel – *Chapel, Chapel, Chapel,* three times on a Sunday, two full services and Sunday School sandwiched between them in the afternoon.

Sunday School! At half past two every Sabbath Day, I'd join a gaggle of small children to be led through the creaking door at the front of Bethel Chapel, and down the dizzyingly steep wooden stairs to the Vestry, a kind of cavernous basement hall. Deep in the bowels of the earth, the Vestry was heated

215

only by a couple of gas fires mounted high on the walls, and those walls were filmed with damp and condensation. It was clammy on the hottest summer's day and freezing in the depths of winter. All the same, it was a cavern of delight. It was here that Auntie Katie would tell us the most amazing stories – stories illustrated by flannelgraph, a kind of primitive form of animation-without-the-movement, using felt cut-out figures of Bible characters which Auntie Katie would press onto an upright easel and board covered with green baize. Noah and his Ark and three or four token pairs of flannelgraph animals hung there precariously whilst the rain descended and the floods came and washed everything else away, Auntie Katie said. Then the rain stopped and, triumphantly, she'd produce a dazzling rainbow, and smooth it into position right above Noah's big boat, an arc above the Ark, if you see what I mean. Auntie Katie was ancient, by the way. She probably knew Shem, Ham and Japheth personally.

Other Bible stories had special songs, 'choruses' they were called, to explain them and make them memorable. How did Moses cross the Red Sea? "God blew with His wind, *puff, puff, puff, puff*; He blew just enough, 'nough, 'nough, 'nough, 'nough" – and the waters parted miraculously. How did the boy called David defeat the giant Philistine, Goliath, armed with nothing but a sling? "Only a boy called David, only a babbling brook. Only a boy called David, five little stones he took. One little stone went into the sling, And the sling went round and round. Round and round, And round and round, And round and round and round. One little stone went up in the air... And the giant came tumbling down!" See, it works! I can still picture it all.

Best of all, of course, were the songs and stories about Jesus, who wanted me for a Sunbeam, so I had to shine out, *sh-sh-sh-shine* for Him. In one of my favourite stories, a rich man named Zacchaeus wanted to get a look at who this Jesus was, as He was passing by one day. Zacchaeus was very rich

– but very short, no taller than us nippers. He couldn't see over the heads of the crowd. So he climbed up a tree to get a better view, and that's where Jesus spotted him. And not only spotted him, according to the chorus we sang, but shouted up, "Zacchaeus, you come down – for I'm coming to your house for tea!"

That song struck a chord with me. After Sunday School, *I* would be on my way to my Nana's house *for tea*, so I could imagine Jesus and Zacchaeus sitting down to jam sandwiches and cracknels, just like us; and after that they'd have tinned peaches and ideal milk and a glass of Dandelion and Burdock – that was bound to be Jesus's favourite flavour, too, I was sure of that. Perhaps He and Zacchaeus even watched *Lost in Space*, if they were allowed to watch TV on Sunday – which *I* wasn't in my own house, but my indulgent Nana let me do.

There was a more serious, grown-up point to the Biblical story – Zaccheus was a corrupt tax-collector, a collaborator with the Romans who'd conquered Israel. Respectable Jews wouldn't have sullied themselves by going to his house. Jesus did, and the upshot was that Zacchaeus promised to give half of his fortune to the poor, and repay everyone he'd cheated four times over.

I didn't get as far as understanding any of that back then; in fact, I probably mixed Zacchaeus up with Dr Zachary Smith, the miserable baddie in *Lost in Space*, who was also in need of redemption.

Back in Sunday School, in the run-up to Christmas, Auntie Katie got her easel out and showed us how the baby Jesus was born. *There* was the Stable. And the Manger. And the Star. And the flannelgraph Mary and Joseph, and the flannelgraph Shepherds and the flannelgraph Angels, all just about hanging on to the green baize, and the little Lord Jesus laying down His sweet head, and also in mortal danger of dropping off, as it were. Thank goodness the Wise Men turned up in time on their Camels with his Christmas presents.

But – as with Zacchaeus – there was another side to the Christmas story, one quite different from the comforting and sentimental version we sang about in *Away in a Manger*, one that was kept from us in our early years in Sunday School, or downplayed at any rate. Mary and Joseph, you see, were effectively homeless when Jesus was born, and then, because King Herod became paranoid and murderous when he heard the Wise Men's prophecy about a *new* king being born, one who might replace him, they had to flee into Egypt. Yes, that's right, Jesus's family were *refugees*, seeking asylum in a foreign land, dependent on the welcome they found amongst strangers. It's worth thinking about, isn't it? How different the whole story might have been if Mary and Joseph hadn't found a safe haven to raise their infant son.

For most of us these days, Christmas is a family time, and despite the way it's been commercialised, it remains precious because of that. During the pandemic, *certain* politicians would have done almost anything to avoid being seen to be 'stealing' or 'cancelling' Christmas – especially, it turns out, if they themselves had been party to parties, when others had been observing lockdown religiously. Indeed, Christmas has become almost sacrosanct in our secular society, in a way that I'm sure is surprising to those who've been marking it faithfully in the old-fashioned Chapel way year after year.

Chapels play a much less prominent part in Rhondda life, in Welsh life, by now. Ebenezer and Calfaria, Ainon and Penuel, Hermon and Horeb, Noddfa and Moriah – they're names that don't trip so easily off the tongue anymore. Many Chapel buildings have been demolished, others adapted for new purposes, quite different to their original use. But, each year, as we prepare for the Season of Goodwill and Joy to All, whether you're raising a glass, or raising a prayer, or doing both, you might like to spare a thought for Auntie Katie and her flannelgraph: for all the lessons we learned when we were small, and for all the ones we still have to learn, however old we are.

43
Trimming the Coalface for Christmas

WHEN DO YOU 'trim up' for Christmas? In the last couple of years, my friends seem to be putting their decorations up earlier and earlier. With the way the world is, I suppose they reckon we need that extra bit of cheer just as soon as we can get it.

'Trimming up'. It's a good old Rhondda phrase for putting up the decorations... on the tree, all through the house and – increasingly, these days – outside it too. If you've never seen Mid-Rhondda in midwinter, you're missing one of the Seven Wonders of modern Wales. Don't bother with an expensive cruise to the Arctic Circle in the hope of glimpsing the Northern Lights. Just head to Tonypandy. The *cwm* will have been transformed into a winter wonderland, terrace above terrace of illuminated Santas, multicoloured sleighs and flashing reindeers lighting up our linear city from end to end.

As I was stringing the perfectly modest set of lights around *my* tree this last December, I was thinking about a letter that I've kept safe for more than 40 years now. It was a treasure worth keeping: *a letter from a listener*.

You see, the most rewarding thing about working in broadcasting is when the audience responds. These days, it's emails or texts, posts on Facebook or that other platform that used to be called Twitter, sometimes a phone call. But back when I began my career, we used to get *handwritten letters*. And this one, in particular... well, you'll see for yourself why I've cherished it ever since, even though it's got a bitter twist in the tail.

Before I get into that, perhaps I'd better explain – since we're nearly at the end of this book – what a boy from Penygraig was doing in the media in the first place. You see, when I was growing up in the 1960s, something astonishing happened to a neighbour of ours: she was interviewed on the BBC! She talked about a local campaign, and everyone else on Tylacelyn Road agreed that what she'd said had been very good. But all the same, the way she'd said it struck them as unfortunate.

"She did sound very *Welsh*, didn't she?" they all agreed.

"What's the matter with that?" I wondered, an indignant 10 year old.

As I got a bit older and turned into a bolshie teenager, I realised that the only reason she'd sounded 'very Welsh' was that, in those days, nobody else on the airwaves did. And I do mean – *literally* – nobody else. You just didn't hear people with working-class Welsh accents like ours on TV or radio. 'Ordinary' people's lives might occasionally be reported on or dramatised; they were never presented first-hand. So it was the *context* which made our neighbour seem uncouth, even to her own kind. And if they thought that *she* didn't belong on the BBC, it must mean that they felt that *they* didn't really belong there either. That what was natural to us was inferior, somehow. I knew that that was wrong. I knew that Rhondda people were as good as anyone else – in fact, I thought they were a good deal better than many of those who did seem to regard it as their birthright to be on the BBC. Not only was it wrong, it was *important*, I realised. Important for our own self-respect, as well as for everyone else if they wanted to understand the world as it really is, for us to be represented – to the wider world and to ourselves – on our own terms.

It was because of all that – because I was indignant and bolshie and stubborn, and wouldn't let something go if I thought it wasn't right and I could do something about it – that I did do something about it. It was my Dad's 'stickability' coming through in me, perhaps. I pushed myself forward when the chance came, and so I found myself, at the grand old age of 21, sitting in a 'mobile studio' (a caravan!) in the De Winton Street Car Park near Tonypandy Square, broadcasting to the whole valley. BBC Radio Rhondda had arrived – and it was everything my teenage self had said that the BBC should be. *Our voices, our accents, our platform to talk about the things that matter to us.* It was a kind of forerunner of Rhondda Radio, the community station where my talks are broadcast today. Back then, the BBC version was only on the air for a week, but in that time, almost everyone in the Rhondda seemed to have tuned in. Perhaps you remember listening yourself. And it helped set up something that was much longer-lasting and more far-reaching. Let me explain.

It was the autumn of 1978. The BBC had – at long last – decided to launch a dedicated national radio station for Wales. It was a big moment. One of Wales's most famous historians, John Davies (born in the Rhondda and brought up in Dumfries Street, Treorchy), points to the launch of Radio Wales as *the* most significant day in the whole history of the BBC in Wales. For the first time, we had an all-day, stand-alone radio service of our own. But a new radio station needs an audience, and to help drum one up, in the weeks immediately before the launch, the BBC sent its mobile studio – that caravan – right into the heart of four communities across the country. Of course, the first of them just had to be the Rhondda.

Back then, a radio station's wavelength was crucial information for the audience. There were no automatic pre-sets or apps. You had to *tune in* to radio stations. You turned the numbered dial until the fuzzy signal changed and came through loud and clear. So every station wanted to make sure you remembered the exact wavelength they were broadcasting on. Radio 1 had a famous jingle advertising its wavelength – *'Radio 1 is wonderful... 247!'*

So when the bosses of **BBC Radio Rhondda** asked bolshie young John Geraint to present an afternoon sequence of bolshie young music aimed at a bolshie young Rhondda audience, I came up with a bit of patter for the show that I thought might be just as catchy. I blush to remember it: *'Radio Rhondda, 202, through with you... till 7 o'clock, this is Rhondda Rock.'*

Getting listeners to retune to a temporary, pop-up station should have been a daunting, nigh on impossible challenge. But Radio Rhondda had a secret weapon: *Rediffusion!* Rediffusion was a cable TV company. Because the valley was so deep and narrow, television signals struggled to reach our aerials. Rediffusion solved the problem by piping *four* TV channels into almost every Rhondda home. What a choice! There was a little Rediffusion box sitting on our living-room windowsill, with an upright switch on top for changing channels. And there were two bonus services you could turn to – radio stations, normally Radio 2 and Radio 4. But step forward Teleri Bevan, the visionary founding Editor of **BBC Radio Wales**. For the week we broadcast Radio Rhondda, Teleri persuaded Rediffusion to drop Radio 2 and carry our programmes instead. Instantly, we had an audience of tens of thousands. And word got around. By the end of the week, it really did feel like everyone in the valley was listening.

When BBC Radio Wales launched a few weeks later, we took the lessons of Radio Rhondda with us. *Radio Wales on the Road* took over the national airwaves for a whole morning every week, 'live' and unedited, with a caravan and a roving radio mic on the streets of Treorchy or Tredegar, Wrexham or Rhyl. It was the format we'd pioneered on Radio Rhondda. Rather than politicians and experts in a fusty old studio, we heard straight from the audience themselves, in the places they lived in: the sound of the real Wales, literally a breath of fresh air.

The audience drawn to this new sound was the one we'd courted on Radio Rhondda – ordinary people, not the 'opinion formers' who were the core listeners to BBC Radio 4 *(apologies if you're one!)*. So when that first December came round for the new Radio Wales, and we asked listeners to write in sharing their stories of Christmas past, one of the letters came from someone who'd been a fan of Radio Rhondda, and had stuck with us on the fledgling national station. He was a proud former miner, William Coombes of the Terraces in Llwynypia. This is how his seasonal story began:

> Never a Christmas comes without one special memory for me of a strange and wonderful moment deep underground. There were some great characters underground in those days. I worked with them for 38 years and I don't think we will see their likes again.

Mr Coombes went on to describe one particular shift with his fellow miners.

> We were at the coalface when the shout came, "Grub up!" We only had 20 minutes, so out came the Tommy Boxes with our bread and cheese. One of the boys was eating a raw onion that stank the place out. Anyway, Christmas was only a week away, and I said, for a joke, "What about trimming the coalface?" Most of them had a good laugh, but the joke stuck with me and my butty, Josh Wilkins. As we walked out at the end of the shift, we decided that however much they laughed at us, we would bring down all the decorations we could get.
>
> Christmas Eve came, and my butty and me went down the pit with the trimmings. It was the afternoon shift and when the other fellows knew what we were up to, they all agreed to get the work done early. We all put our backs into it, jobs like

prop drawing and clearing the coal from the face. Everything went according to plan and the time came to trim the coalface. We had the old electric lamps at that time. We hung them on wooden supports and put coloured paper through the lamp glasses. Then we dangled the trimmings from one pit prop to another. In the darkness of the mine, the effect was wonderful. It was the prettiest sight I've ever seen. And to finish it all off we sat down and sang carols. It was something I shall never forget. That Christmas Eve had a magic touch about it.

And then, right at the bottom of the page, William Coombes wrote one final line – simple, heartbreaking, devastating. Because, yes, the pit where all this happened was the Cambrian Colliery in Clydach Vale.

'Ten years later,' wrote Mr Coombes, 'in 1965, many of my pals were killed in an explosion at the colliery.'

And that was it. The camaraderie and the characterfulness, the toughness and the tenderness, the beauty and the tragedy of Rhondda's mining experience, of so much of the Rhondda's whole story, expressed with native eloquence in the span of one short letter. A letter, of course, that we shared on air with the whole of Wales. And now that I've written a hundred letters of my own – because that's what each episode of *John on the Rhondda* is, a *love letter* to my valley – it seems fitting to end here.

Rhondda's history, Rhondda's values, the tales we've told each other, the songs we've sung, the terraces and *gwlis* we've all trudged up and down, the hills and mountains we've walked, the chapels and pubs we've gone to, the cinemas and schools and fields we've played in, the work we've done, the people we've cared for, the way we've come together to fight for what's right, the camaraderie that makes us *us* – all of that has forged the Rhondda's unique character, and made it such a special place.

William Coombes was right: we'll never see the likes of him and his butties again. But there is *something* in that shared experience, in the way that Rhondda men and women have lived – something I've tried to represent and celebrate in the radio and TV programmes that I've made, and in these talks and podcasts – something that we need to hang onto, not out of any sentimental attachment to the past, but because it's a glimpse of something humanity has always been searching for; because it points to a way of living that's *fair shares* and *fair do's* for everybody, a world we can all enjoy the better, because it's better for all of us.

Yes, it's the promise of that Promised Land: of yet to come, none the less true. I can see it, shimmering in the distance. For all that's changed, in the Rhondda and the wider world, we can reach it still.

Postscript: Legacy, Heritage and History

SINCE I PUT this collection of reflections together – and recorded the hundredth episode of *John on the Rhondda* – we've received some very welcome news at Rhondda Radio. An application we made to the National Lottery Heritage Fund has been successful. The Heritage Fund has awarded us a major grant, recognising that – as proud as Rhondda people are of their past – 30 years after the last piece of coal was raised in the valley, and nearly 70 years since William Coombes and his butties 'trimmed up' the Cambrian coalface for Christmas, the Rhondda's industrial inheritance is in danger of falling into forgetfulness.

The Heritage Fund grant will enable us to do three things. First, to create a Rhondda Heritage Trail, a physical reality running through twelve 'stations' at significant locations up and down the Fach and the Fawr (in the tram tracks, as I like to think, of those electric streetcars which – as long ago as the decade that saw the First World War – sped the citizens of this linear city the whole length of our twin valleys).

Secondly, we're going to mount a year-long 'festival' of broadcast programmes on Rhondda Radio, celebrating our rich history. As Creative Director of the project, I'm determined to involve all ages in that, and particularly the Rhondda's schoolchildren.

Indeed, the third strand of our project will be to train a new generation of Rhondda broadcasters, an 'on-air' legacy for Rhondda Radio. This should strengthen its role as a voice for the valley.

So Legacy, Heritage and History – those three key words are much in my mind these days. Whole academic careers have been spent defining them. But, in my simple way, I like to picture them in terms of *a cloak*, one of those beautifully woven cloaks I imagine the heroes and heroines of the *Mabinogion* wearing, perhaps. *Legacy* is the cloak that's been handed down to us from previous generations. *Heritage* is the way we wear that cloak, the pride we feel as it adorns our shoulders. And *History*? History is how that cloak was made, and why – not just the bald facts of its manufacture, but what it meant to those who crafted it, and what it means to us now.

But Legacy is also what we hand down to *our* children and grandchildren, the Heritage we bequeath to them, the History we teach them. It's time for my generation to pass that cloak on. Soon, it may be refashioned in a style more fitting for tomorrow's world. But the stuff it's made of, at least in the peculiar sort of *hiraeth* of my forward-looking imagination – that will always, always be *the Rhondda*, through and through.

Acknowledgements

I'M TRULY GRATEFUL to the team at Rhondda Radio. It's a community service, run by volunteers, free-to-air in the valley and available online worldwide, which first gave me a platform to reach an audience with these talks. Special thanks are due to David Arthur, a talented broadcaster and a generous soul, who's hosted *John on the Rhondda* weekly on his afternoon show. David has been unfailingly encouraging and supportive from the off. And his jokes are *almost* as good mine. They're in the same class, at any rate.

Diolch i Carolyn Hodges, my brilliant and insightful editor at Y Lolfa, for seeing the potential to turn these spoken 'sermons' into print, and for helping me to realise that potential in the best way that I can.

Most of all, I need to acknowledge the working-class institutions and the people of the Rhondda, whose character, achievements and principles are the bedrock of everything that's written here. Many of my Rhondda friends and family are named in the book, and others who aren't have been just as influential. In particular, I'd like to thank my cousins, Susan and Desmond Jones, who have lived all their married lives in a house I've mentioned several times here: the house that was my grandparents' home in Holborn Terrace, Tonypandy. Susan and Des have always been for me touchstones for all that's good and genuine about our native valley.

This book is dedicated to my parents, the late Margaret and David Roberts. Many Rhondda people would remember them, and fondly. I've held back from writing at length about them in this volume, but – if it's of interest – you could search out, in the long list of my *John on the Rhondda* podcasts, the two whole episodes (subtitled 'The Rhondda Mam' and, simply, 'Dad') which try to express the love and gratitude I feel towards them and for everything they did for me.

My children, Seán, Anwen and Róisín, have heard the majority of the stories and almost all the wisecracks before. Repeatedly. Thanks to them for their patience, and for all they've taught me.

The final credit goes, as always, to a woman who was born far from the Rhondda, but who can't be faulted in any other respect: my wife, the wonderfully gifted Angela Graham.

John Geraint
November 2023

JOHN ON THE RHONDDA

The *John on the Rhondda* podcast,
on which this book is based,
is available free of charge on

Spotify

Apple Podcasts

Google Podcasts

RadioPublic

Pocket Casts

and other platforms.

Also from Y Lolfa:

£9.99

Collection of essays and speeches by historian, political activist and former MP Hywel Francis, celebrating the struggles of the working class in the Valleys.

PubLife

Rhondda Valleys Life
Through Pubs and Clubs, Past and Present

Peter Roberts

y Lolfa

£9.99

A revealing and humorous trawl through the drinking establishments past and present of the Rhondda.

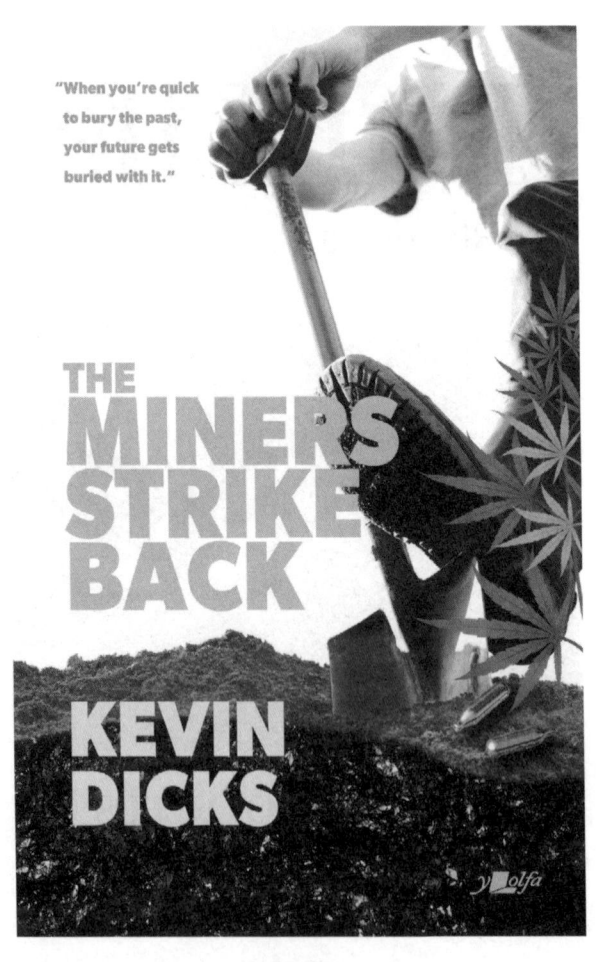

"When you're quick to bury the past, your future gets buried with it."

THE MINERS STRIKE BACK

KEVIN DICKS

£9.99

Widowed ex-miner Johnny finds coal on his allotment and battles to keep his tiny colliery secret in an increasingly hostile green world.

Jac
Sam Adams

£9.99

Coming-of-age novel set in a south Wales mining valley, following the escapades of a group of boys growing up during World War II.

WELSH VALLEYS PHRASEBOOK
GET BY IN VALLEYS-SPEAK!

David Jandrell

£3.99

A humorous guide to and phrasebook of Valleys-speak, affectionately poking fun at the grammar, slang terms and culture of the Valleys.

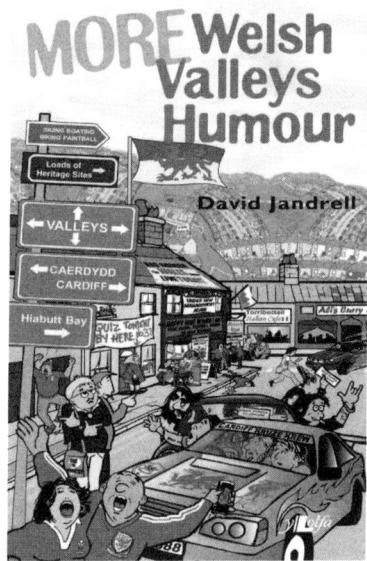

£3.95 each

Two tongue-in-cheek collections of the unique humour of the Valleys. Including cartoons, and foreword by Ronnie Barker.

> "Simply one of the great characters of Welsh and British rugby." **MAX BOYCE**

FOREWORD BY **SIR GARETH EDWARDS**

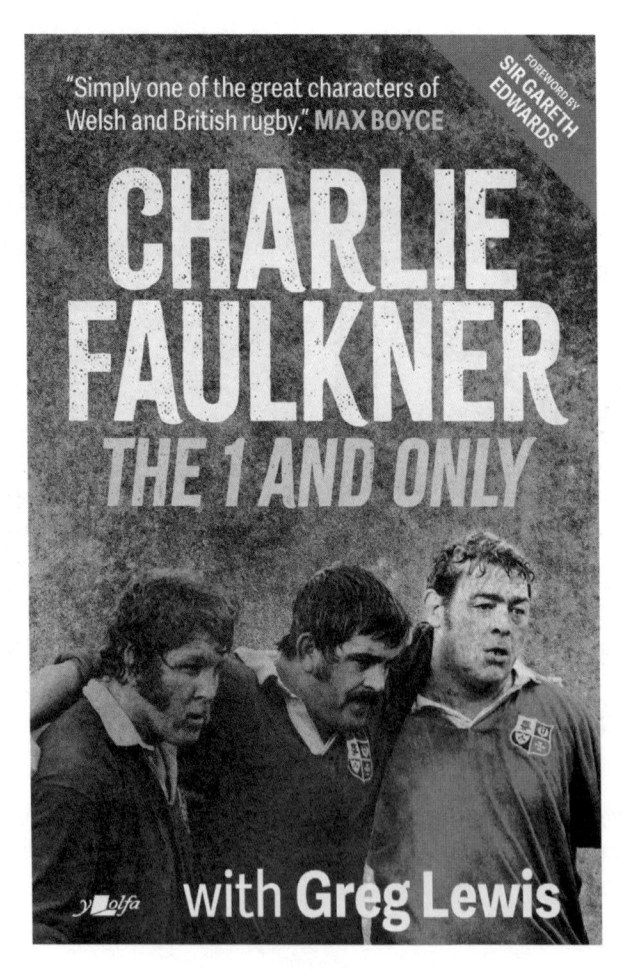

CHARLIE FAULKNER
THE 1 AND ONLY

with **Greg Lewis**

£9.99

Autobiography of key member of the renowned 'Pontypool Front Row, and of the 1970s Golden Era Wales rugby team.

RUGBY LIVES

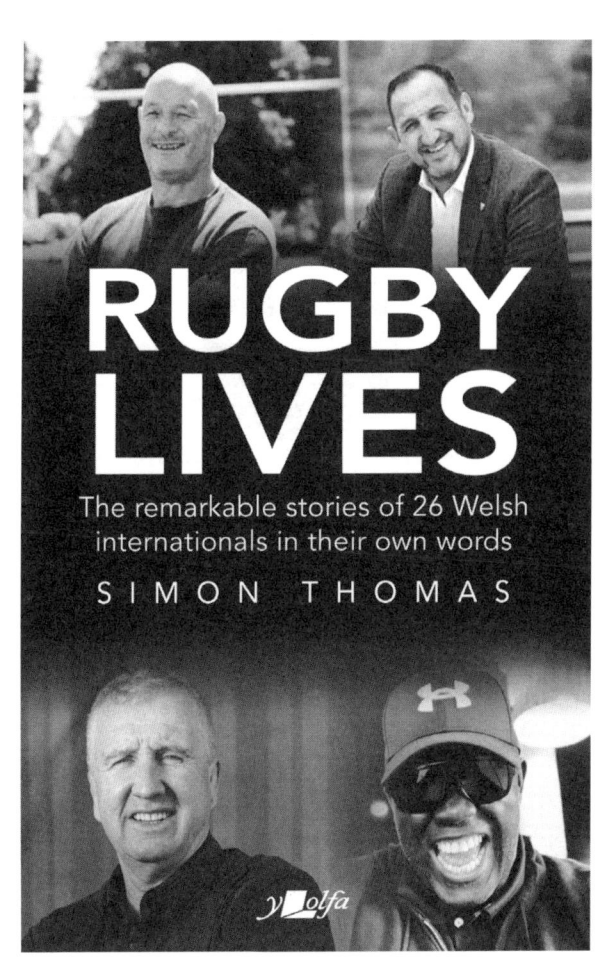

The remarkable stories of 26 Welsh internationals in their own words

SIMON THOMAS

£12.99

A collection of in-depth interviews with 26 of Welsh rugby's finest players, from one of Wales' best rugby journalists.